Clausewitz in His Time

Clausewitz in His Time
Essays in the Cultural and Intellectual History of Thinking about War

Peter Paret

berghahn
NEW YORK • OXFORD
www.berghahnbooks.com

Published by
Berghahn Books
www.berghahnbooks.com

© 2015 Peter Paret

All rights reserved. Except for the quotation of short passages for the purposes of criticism and review, no part of this book may be reproduced in any form or by any means, electronic or mechanical, including photocopying, recording, or any information storage and retrieval system now known or to be invented, without written permission of the publisher.

Library of Congress Cataloging-in-Publication Data

Paret, Peter.
   Clausewitz in his time : essays in the cultural and intellectual history of thinking about war / Peter Paret. — First edition.
      pages cm
   Includes bibliographical references and index.
     ISBN 978-1-78238-581-3 (hardback : alk. paper) — ISBN 978-1-78238-582-0 (ebook)
 1. Clausewitz, Carl von, 1780–1831—Influence. 2. Clausewitz, Carl von, 1780–1831. 3. Military art and science—History. 4. War (Philosophy)—History. I. Title.
  U43.R9.P37 2015
  355.02—dc23
                                                       2014019633

British Library Cataloguing in Publication Data

A catalogue record for this book is available from the British Library

Printed on acid-free paper.

ISBN 978-1-78238-581-3 hardback
ISBN 978-1-78238-582-0 ebook

Contents

Acknowledgments	vi
Introduction	1
1. Text and Context: Two Paths to Clausewitz	5
2. A Learned Officer among Others	18
3. Frederick the Great as Interpreted by Clausewitz and Schlieffen: Three Phases in the History of Strategy	77
4. From Ideal to Ambiguity: Johannes von Müller, Clausewitz, and the People in Arms	87
5. "Half against My Will, I Have Become a Professor"	100
6. Two Historians on Defeat in War and Its Causes	113
Bibliography	127
Index of Texts	131
Name Index	133

Illustrations follow page 76.

Acknowledgments

The four previously published essays—now revised and somewhat expanded—in this collection of old and new studies on Clausewitz, are reprinted with the kind permission of the editors of the publications in which they first appeared: the third essay under the slightly different title "Clausewitz and Schlieffen as Interpreters of Frederick the Great: Three Phases in the History of Grand Strategy," in *Journal of Military History* 76 (2012); the fourth essay on the ideal conception and the realistic understanding of the "people in arms" in *Journal of the History of Ideas* 65, no. 1 (2004); the fifth essay combines new material with the documentation and interpretation in three earlier talks and essays: "Clausewitz' Vorlesungen über den Kleinen Krieg an der Neuen Kriegsschule in Berlin, 1810–1812," which opened a conference on the history of officer education at the Humboldt University in Berlin, and was published in the *Jahrbuch der Clausewitz Gesellschaft* 6 (2011); "Clausewitz: Half against My Will, I Have Become a Professor," in *Journal of Military History* 75 (April 2011); and "Aufklärung und Preussische Reform: Clausewitz' Vorlesungen über den Kleinen Krieg," in *Ideenpolitik–Festschrift für Herfried Münkler,* ed. Harald Blum et al., Berlin, 2012. The sixth essay, comparing interpretations of defeat by Clausewitz and Marc Bloch, which was awarded the 2010 Jack Miller Center Prize of the Historical Society, appeared in *Historically Speaking* 11 (June 2010).

I am indebted to Ulrich Raulff, director of the Schiller Nationalmuseum and the Deutsche Literaturarchiv, who generously placed the resources of his institution at my disposal; to Marcia Tucker and her staff of the Historical Studies and Social Science Library of the Institute for Advanced Study for the ready assistance I received from them in this most recent project, as in others previously; to my daughter Suzanne Aimée Paret who succeeded in photographing Rauch's statue of Scharnhorst in Berlin, even though the area was closed for construction; and to Henning Köhler of the Freie Universität Berlin, who helped in locating bibliographical material. Once again I greatly benefitted from the comments and criticism of my son Paul and of four colleagues who generously gave their time to read sections of the manuscript: Lionel Gossman and Walter H. Hinderer, both of Princeton University; Hans

Joachim Kreutzer of the University of Regensburg , the long-time president of the Heinrich von Kleist Gesellschaft; and John W. Shy of the University of Michigan. For information kindly volunteered I also want to express my gratitude to Vanya Eftimova Bellinger, who is working on newly available letters of Marie von Clausewitz, and to Bernd Domsgen and Olaf Thiel of the Freundeskreis Clausewitz in Clausewitz's birthplace Burg near Magdeburg, an association of local historians that is collecting valuable information, above all on Clausewitz's parents and on his early life. Finally, I want to thank Kristine Hunt for her restrained copy editing, and Elizabeth Berg, Adam Capitanio, and Melissa Spinelli for the care with which they saw the manuscript through the press.

Introduction

The six essays in this volume—some new, some previously published and now revised—review Clausewitz's life, his theories, and the links between them, with particular attention to the culture and thought of his time. The first two studies, both new, together well over half of the text, take a general, comprehensive view of Clausewitz's life and work. The first discusses Clausewitz as a historical figure, an individual marked by the conditions and events of his time, whose ideas nevertheless continue to have something to say to the present, even as they confront today's reader with challenges that may not always be fully recognized. The second essay, focused on his life, expands the usual biographical perspective. Rather than largely concentrating on Clausewitz, it sees him in connection with several other individuals, and considers their lives and work together: The essay follows Clausewitz as the student of a teacher who was to exert a lasting influence on him, and then as one of five officers, all born within the same years and linked for decades in their careers and intellectual interests, an approach that by focusing on so far unexplored relationships leads to new information that broadens and deepens our knowledge of Clausewitz's biography, and in turn casts additional light on the development of his ideas and theories. The four previously published essays that follow address particular issues in his life, and in the development of his ideas. They are case studies that relate to and complement the preceding general discussion by examining such issues as Clausewitz's analysis of popular or revolutionary war, the attention he gives to psychological elements in war, ranging from soldiers' fear in combat to the personal characteristics of supreme commanders, and the place political motives occupy in his theory of war. Soldiers and military and political thinkers of his time took the political purposes of war for granted, as their successors do today, but Clausewitz found a way to integrate this matter-of-fact recognition into a comprehensive analysis that seeks ideological objectivity in his analysis of political and military reality as he develops a more expansive role of politics, not only as the source and goal of war, but also as one of the determinants—together with social, intellectual, and technological factors—of its course and its methods.

Having outlined some of the major issues addressed in the following essays, I should say a few words about the scholarly motives that drive them. The six essays continue the study of Clausewitz, his writings, his times, and the literature concerning him and his work that I began in 1965 with two articles, a bibliographical overview and a very preliminary outline of his place in the history of military theory.[1] The two pieces had a descriptive predecessor, a few pages on Clausewitz and defensive popular war in the historical section of a short book on the political, social, and military characteristics of guerrilla warfare that John W. Shy and I, then both in an early phase of studying and teaching history, published in 1962.[2] Our research on eighteenth- and early nineteenth-century issues had extended to episodes of the "little war" of popular uprisings, and to similarities and differences between a number of conflicts of this kind, past and current. With our interpretations of the predecessors of the new revolutionary wars, we hoped to expand the historical perspective of the strategic debate of the 1950s and 1960s, which sought a way through the dual mazes of nuclear war and ideologically driven irregular conflicts. But even in those days my wish to acquire an understanding of *On War* beyond the impressions gained in early readings of Clausewitz's formidable work was motivated less by present-day political and strategic issues than by a strong historical interest in the author and his life—at first concentrated on his participation in the reforms of the Prussian Army after the rout of ancien régime Prussia and its army in the War of 1806, the subject of my doctoral dissertation, then expanding to Clausewitz's political and historical writings, and increasingly to his effort to develop an objective, systematically analytic view of war. From the start, his concern with war as one of the major phenomena in history attracted me not only for his ideas as such, but also for their links with—or reactions against—aspects of the culture and thought beyond the military reality of his time, which directly or more remotely had a bearing on his analyses.

My occupation with Clausewitz and his theoretical writings, and the dissatisfaction several colleagues and I felt with the existing English texts of *On War*, led to the idea of attempting a new translation, a task that, once begun, was to engage Michael Howard and me for years. It soon came to constitute an unexpectedly demanding background—distant thunder accompanying sunny days—to our work on other subjects, in my case cultural history centered largely though not entirely on German literature and the visual arts, even as my service in an infantry battalion in the South Pacific during the Second World War continued to leave me curious and troubled about war in all its forms, and not least about its place in history. In these years, and with some interruptions, I also wrote a biography of Clausewitz, which appeared in 1976, the same year that Howard and I at last published our translation of *On War*.[3] Eventually this was followed by a translation of selections of Clausewitz's historical and political writings.[4] That might have put an end to my occupation with Clausewitz; but the translations and the biography raised new questions and opened up new topics that called for responses and further work. As an example, in a review of the biography, C.B.A. Behrens disagreed with my appraisal of Clausewitz's political stance in the post-Napoleonic era.[5] In his support of ministerial responsibility and a limited franchise in Prussia, Clausewitz's position seemed to me not too distant from the views of British moderate Whigs before the passage of the Reform Bill of 1832. That British political thought and institutions, as well as the possible lines of future political development in the United Kingdom, differed considerably from those in Prussia was obvious; yet affinities also existed, and it seemed worthwhile to go beneath the labels. After Ms. Behren's review appeared, I had the good fortune while working in the British Museum to come across dispatches of George Henry Rose, after 1815 the British Minister in Berlin, in which he reported that the Prussian monarch and his closest advisors deemed Clausewitz politically unreliable, some going so far as to consider him a liberal. The dispatches and other documents also revealed that Rose, a solid Tory, shared the king's suspicions that Clausewitz had liberal sympathies, and that his conviction drove him to mobilize the Austrian, French, and Russian ambassadors in Berlin to join him and Prussian conservatives in urging Frederick William III not to pursue the suggestion of the Prussian foreign minister to appoint Clausewitz as Prussian ambassador to the Court of St. James. Clausewitz's skeptical view of the ideals and practices of monarchical absolutism, barely masked in post-Napoleonic Germany by some limited representative institutions, were unsuited, they believed, for a diplomatic appointment, and his presence in London was likely to interfere with the good relations of the major powers. In an article I published the documents and my interpretation of this episode in Clausewitz's life, the political maneuvers of which extended over a longer period and engaged him more fully than I at first recognized.[6]

Over the years, as further documents on Clausewitz's life and work were recovered, as more of his published and unpublished texts were reconstructed in modern scholarly editions, notably by the unremitting archival and editorial efforts of Werner Hahlweg, as even a few hitherto unknown Clausewitz letters were found, and I was able to identify a brief anonymous political article in the German press as having been written by him, new causal links and influences became apparent. I pursued some of the newly raised issues, and published the findings in separate studies. The corrections, new information, and expanded interpretations contained in these essays were added as compressed notes to revised editions of the biography; in 1992 a number of my shorter studies on Clausewitz were also reprinted and published as a group.[7] Like these studies, the six essays now appearing in this volume are additions to the already existing biographical framework, and together will, I hope, constitute a further step forward in the continuing exploration of Clausewitz's life, his theoretical and historical writings, and of his cultural, social, and political world, a world that in its nonmilitary as much as in its military aspects has a great deal to tell us not only about his biography and the development of his ideas on war, but also about the nature of these ideas, and the extent of their power to transcend the centuries.

Notes

1. Peter Paret, "Clausewitz: A Bibliographical Survey," *World Politics* 17 (January 1965); Peter Paret, "Clausewitz and the Nineteenth Century," in *The Theory and Practice of War*, ed. Michael Howard (London, 1965).
2. Peter Paret and John W. Shy, *Guerrillas in the 1960s* (New York, 1962), 11-15.
3. Carl von Clausewitz, *On War*, ed. and trans. Michael Howard and Peter Paret (Princeton, 1976, rev. ed. 1984); Peter Paret, *Clausewitz and the State* (New York, 1976, rev. and expanded eds. Princeton, 1985, 2007).
4. Carl von Clausewitz, *Historical and Political Writings,* ed. and trans. Peter Paret and Daniel Moran (Princeton, 1992).
5. C.A.B. Behrens, "Which Side Was Clausewitz on?" *New York Review of Books,* October 14, 1976.
6. Peter Paret, "Bemerkungen zu dem Versuch von Clausewitz zum Gesandten in London ernannt zu werden," *Jahrbuch für die Geschichte Mittel- und Ostdeutschlands* 26 (1977); English translation, "'A Proposition Not a Solution'—Clausewitz's Attempt to Become Prussian Minister at the Court of St. James,'" in Peter Paret, *Understanding War: Essays on Clausewitz and the History of Military Power,* Princeton, 1992.
7. Ibid., 1992.

1

Text and Context
Two Paths to Clausewitz

The text of *On War* and the context in which the work was written, the social, cultural, and political environment as defined by Clausewitz's experiences, are two separate subjects of study, even as each bears on the other.[1] The biographical information contained in Clausewitz's letters and service documents, and in the correspondence and memoirs of contemporaries, followed by the findings of nearly two centuries of research and interpretation, tell us a great deal, if still not as much as we would like, of his life and the stages in which he erected the structure of his theoretical perception of war. New perspectives on his life and work continue to open. But even in our present state of knowledge, Clausewitz's biography casts much light on the development of his thought and often serves as a useful commentary on segments of his work. *On War*, in turn, contains numerous references to the author's experiences. Despite its tone, which may seem impersonal to the modern reader, the book is anything but a detached, formal, narrowly specialized treatise on an obtuse subject. It is hardly necessary to say this about a work that began to attract wide attention soon after it was published, and that, as an international classic born of the world's apparent inability to avoid the use of violence in the relations between states and social groups, continues to be discussed for its contribution to an understanding of war itself, of wars in history, and in the mind of many of its readers today above all for its relevance to contemporary war. Even if Clausewitz had not written *On War*, however, historians would have had cause to pay attention to his life, his political and military activities in the Napoleonic era, his very extensive historical writings that are not only essential foundations for his theoretical work, but also impressive forerunners of the development of the historical sciences in the nineteenth century, and his political writings, which give voice to an interesting, far from common point of view in the political and social history of Prussia between the Napoleonic era and the European revolutions of 1830. References and allusions to each of these issues and activities that engaged Clausewitz can be found in *On War*, which among much else is an intellectual summary of the concerns and ideas that lent impetus to an active, creative life.

Is it easier to combine the facts of Clausewitz's biography into a sequential, meaningful whole than to gain a command of the many arguments in *On War*, a work that demands more analytic agility from its readers than is sometimes recognized? Perhaps—yet biography is an imperfect mode. It rarely if ever fully grasps and reflects, depicts and interprets a life in all its essentials, no matter how extensive the available documents. Both Clausewitz's biography and his theories, in their respective strengths and uncertainties, will continue to test the interpreter. Even as we follow the links between his work and the record and account of his life and see how often one contributes to our understanding of the other, each continues to present significant challenges.

The difficulties *On War* poses to the interpreter and the reader increase with the passage of time. In this connection it may be worth noting that the literature on Clausewitz falls into two somewhat separate groups: studies of his life and studies of his work, his histories but primarily his theories. Recent publications on the theoretical parts of his work may be further divided into interpretations of the theories as such, and the investigation of their pertinence to wars of the early twenty-first century—subjects that in many studies overlap. Today more books and articles are written on the viability of *On War* under modern technological and political conditions, than on aspects of Clausewitz's biography, on his historical writings, or even on his theories seen from a nonutilitarian point of view that concentrates on the realism and logic of his ideas and on their place in the military, political, and intellectual history of late eighteenth- and early nineteenth-century Europe. To be sure, some students of the current relevance of *On War* attempt to measure and incorporate in their conclusions the effects created by the increasing distance between the work's inception and the present; but even those of today's defense analysts who are knowledgeable in the history of war at the junction of the eighteenth and nineteenth centuries will find building the passage of time into their analyses a process that constantly edges into areas other than war, into politics, society, and culture. Another and more important part of the problem may be that they search for something other than Clausewitz has to offer. It is useful to return to basics, and remind ourselves of Clausewitz's intentions, that, as the title of his posthumous works, *Hinterlassene Werke über Krieg und Kriegführung*, makes clear, he writes not only about the conduct of war, but about war itself.

In *On War* Clausewitz develops a systematic, theoretical recognition of the purpose, means, and dynamic of his subject. His ultimate aim is to formulate an understanding of war that is not limited by the conditions of his own time, nor those of any period in history, but one that recognizes how war as part of a larger system of sociopolitical decision and action functioned in the past, is used and waged in his own day, and is likely to function in the future. Within the constantly changing means and methods of organized violence, Clausewitz identifies what he regards as the fundamental elements of war, factors that potentially are always present though they will take many different forms; he measures their actions and interactions, and illustrates these permanent components of violent encounters between political and social entities with references to specific strategic, operational, and even tactical events in the history of warfare. He corrects what he takes to be erroneous opinions about specifics of war and about war itself, opinions often based on the persuasive yet always circumscribed experience of participants or observers, on subjective impressions reinforced by the natural and common tendency to generalize from one's inevitably limited encounters with surface phenomena. Conscious of the difficulties of devising an analytic method that is both objective and reaches to the fundamentals of the subject, he attempts to create a coherent and comprehensive analysis that enables him—and may help enable his readers, critics, and interpreters as they engage with his arguments—to think realistically both about the specifics and the whole of conflicts at present and in the past, and about war as a general phenomenon.[2]

To note that Clausewitz's aim of understanding war includes responding to and criticizing and correcting views he regards as mistaken, is merely another way of saying that he writes not in a vacuum, but in the context of events and ideas to which he is exposed—and in this connection it may not be beside the point to recall that when, at the age of twenty-five, he published his first article it was a harshly critical review of another man's strategic theories.[3] Of the ideas, old and new, that he encounters, many are reflected in his own writings, touching him positively or negatively, with greater or lesser immediacy. *On War,* like any work, however original, is marked by the political, social, and cultural characteristics, present and past, of the times in which the author lives. And similarly, as is true of most books, *On War* is affected by the course of its author's life from childhood to maturity. As his manuscript even before publication takes on an existence of its own, the work remains a part of his life, a life that holds explanations for the thoughts and actions of the person living it, which, in turn, are relevant to the work.

That Clausewitz's analysis of war as an important expression of social and political energy is rooted in both a general and a personal context, does not, of course, restrict his thoughts to the circumstances of his life and of the times in which he wrote. Ideas can rise to define and convey values that transcend the conditions from which they emerged. Even then, however, their origin remains relevant to their content and development, to the course of an idea from its first emergence to its definitive formulation, which subsequently may undergo further refinement, as happened when Clausewitz reached a fuller understanding of the reality and implications of limited war. In the extended sense here suggested, the context in which Clausewitz worked offers a key to phases of his thinking.

That does not mean that one must be a historian of his period or a biographer of his life to be critically receptive of his work in its final state—the reaction Clausewitz hoped for from his readers. In their ultimate form, even though he did not complete the planned revisions of *On War*, his theories are, on the whole, clearly defined and consistent in their content. They, or some part or parts of them, may be self-explanatory. If at times they seem particularly complex, readers throughout recorded history have shown themselves able to extract the matter that interests them even from texts originating in historical and cultural surroundings very different than theirs. One need not be a contemporary of Montesquieu or Kant, to mention two authors whose work left impressions on Clausewitz's theories, nor a historian of eighteenth-century ideas, to grasp the theses of the *Esprit des Lois* or of the *Kritik der reinen Vernunft*. The main and lasting messages of these books stand on their own, even if aspects and details surrounding them will remain obscure to readers without a knowledge of the history, conditions, and thought of the times in which their authors lived. What does, however, seem desirable, indeed essential, is for those of today's readers who seek contemporary relevance in the works of Montesquieu, Kant, or Clausewitz, to keep in mind that they are not reading the thoughts of a judge, philosopher, or soldier of their own day, that even ideas retaining a force across the centuries were at their creation formulated differently than they would be today, and that some of their implications, even aspects of their meanings, may have changed since they were first written.

If an understanding of Clausewitz's text may be affected by the context in which it was written, the nature of his subject and his manner of approaching it can also create difficulties. Although in *On War* Clausewitz emphasizes that "theory should be study, not doctrine," his intentions are not always fully recognized, or if recognized easily accepted.[4] Even if utilitarian motives originally led him to his theoretical work, and are rarely wholly absent for long, he is basically driven not by the wish to win wars, but the need to understand war, from its political and even social origins to actions in the field and to the impact of these actions on the military, political, and often social outcome. To think of war along the lines he develops may contribute to effectiveness in practice, even if superior knowledge has never assured effective leadership. In a sphere as pragmatically oriented as the study of war, intellect and knowledge function only if driven by appropriate psychological energy. Some readers and interpreters may nevertheless find it difficult to conceive of theoretical explorations that are not immediately directed at practical results—especially if such hoped-for returns are what initially brought them to Clausewitz. However unambiguous his statement of purpose, they expect his principal intention to be, after all, utilitarian—the development of strategic and operational concepts that apply certainly to his day, but directly or indirectly may also possess relevance for the readers' own time. Such misunderstandings or even willful misreadings may be further encouraged by the fact that *On War* combines theoretical analysis with strategic, operational, occasionally even tactical discussions, and contains as well many shorter references to campaigns during the author's life and in earlier centuries. Certainly, in *On War* Clausewitz does not hesitate to state his opinions of the actions he discusses at length, or more often outlines in a few sentences. But the primary function of these references to success and failure is not to support a particular doctrine. Rather they offer examples of similar as well as changing forms that war assumed over time, which is the object of his analysis. "Whenever the thread of my argument became too thin," he writes in a preliminary study for *On War*, I have preferred to break it off and go back to the relevant phenomena of experience."[5] Summaries of past events are segments of reality that frame the exposition of his theory.

A further and very understandable reason readers may expect to encounter a pragmatic orientation in *On War* can be found in Clausewitz's military career, a career, consisting mainly though not wholly of staff and administrative appointments, that caused him to write a vast number of reports, memoranda, lectures, and notes, evidence of which reappears in *On War*. In the course of thirty-nine years in the Prussian army Clausewitz held positions that in peacetime gave him a voice in the development or critique of doctrine, and in war some influence on operations in the field. As one of the officers most actively engaged in the politics of reforming the Prussian army after its defeat in the War of 1806, and as a staff officer in the Wars of Liberation, he concentrated on increasing and maintaining the effectiveness of the forces in which he served, although even then he introduced other motives into the military considerations at issue—for example, his advocacy of the introduction of universal military service and of opening officer commissions to broader segments of society is joined to arguments for turning the inertly obedient subject of the state into a citizen and reducing or eliminating some of the legally imposed differences in rights and privileges between groups of the population—changes he urged not only on military but also on sociopolitical grounds. In contrast to his historical and theoretical works, in which he strove for objectivity with a determination that could confuse or irritate readers for whom partisanship was a more natural and expected attitude, the reports and memoranda he wrote in the service and the lectures he gave between 1810 and 1812 at the new War Academy in Berlin are pragmatic in nature and tone. To the officer on active service the issue of immediate effectiveness was dominant. To the scholar and theorist victory in a battle or a war was one matter among others.

But, it may be objected, even if Clausewitz's principal intention was not the development of a strategic system of more than temporary validity or even of validity today, might he not at least be seen as a proponent and codifier of Napoleonic warfare? In his campaigns the emperor mobilized and successfully applied the energies generated by the most centralized political, administrative, and military system of his day. Innovations in military policy brought about by the French Revolution, measures that resulted from social and political changes in France, but also affected methods of discipline, training, and ways of fighting, helped him create a newly large and integrated military instrument that under his leadership overwhelmed its opponents with offensives of unusual power, rapidity, and range. More than once—and particularly in the general literature—Clausewitz has been read and discussed as the "intellectual inheritor" of Napoleonic warfare.[6] If this is to mean that Clausewitz was not only an analyst of strategy and operations in the Napoleonic era, but regarded the emperor's practices as the system according to which war was now to be waged, and furthermore provided this system with its theoretical underpinnings, the characterization is mistaken. Certainly, the wars from the early 1790s to 1815 never ceased to stimulate Clausewitz's thinking. They were a major part of his life. He narrated and analyzed the wars, their strategic characteristics and their battles in some of the most refined historical interpretations of the time, and even as he opposed Napoleon and searched for weaknesses in his character and policies, he never questioned the emperor's brilliance. In *On War* he often refers to his campaigns. But that it was not Clausewitz's principal intention to encode Napoleonic warfare is already indicated by his still more numerous references in *On War* to other wars from antiquity to the wars of Frederick the Great and of the first years of the French Revolution—the purpose of the references being to understand the reasons, good or bad, these actions were taken, not to show Napoleon's superiority; all marking and illustrating basic elements of war as they shape events. And so far as the lasting supremacy of the Napoleonic system is concerned, its opponents, Clausewitz among them, demonstrated clearly enough between 1812 and 1815 that the emperor could be defeated. Nor was it a matter of Napoleon's opponents following a single system that proved superior to his. In the organization and use of their forces they differed from him, but also among themselves.

In one respect, nevertheless, Clausewitz's theories were not only affected, but may have been liberated by the Napoleonic experience, which returns us to the role context played in the development of his work. To defeat the new practices in war at the end of the eighteenth century required more than adjustments and even radical change in the military institutions and administrative policies of the European powers; to greater or lesser degree in the various armies it also demanded new ways of using forces in the field. Eighteenth-century strategic and operational doctrine, which since the Seven Years' War, especially in the armies of Central Europe, had become increasingly systematic and prescriptive, was now confronted by methods that overwhelmed the familiar pattern. Yet at first the common response to the new dynamic in warfare and its rejection of earlier standards and conventions was not greater flexibility but—excepting for small tactical adjustments—more complex and prescriptive doctrines, which were influenced by new theories finding support in quasi-mathematical rules on such matters as the "correct" angle for advancing from an operational base to the tactical objective. Examples are the publications of Bülow and Jomini, two intelligent and imaginative theorists, who recognized that changes in the conduct of operations were needed, and devised strategic and operational systems, which, though greatly differing from each other, were alike in prescribing patterns of action and response covering a range of strategic and operational eventualities. Their common weakness was to turn their understanding of current flaws and opportunities into keys for permanent success. Clausewitz, on the contrary—very early on, if we can judge from documents to be discussed in the following essay (the answer to a test written in his years at the Berlin Institute for Young Officers, his first historical manuscripts, and his very critical review, written at the age of twenty-five, of one of Bülow's books), came to suspect the value of systems of fixed responses based on unchanging principles, doubts that soon turned to lasting certainty. Throughout his life he was to separate himself—seriously, at times ironically—from generals who lived by the authority of manual and doctrine. As he saw it, they took insufficient account of the uncertainty that is fundamental to war, and to possibilities that were difficult to quantify and fit into their prescriptive systems—if they considered them at all. An obvious example of the uncertain would be an opposing general, whose peculiar way of thinking, backed by imagination and energy, could disrupt any expected pattern of action and response—in short, a Napoleon. In their own fashion, the dogmatic teachings of these modern system-builders were as inadequate as the now outdated practices of the ancien régime they attempted to replace. And it may be that the belief in and search for systems promising victory, widespread at the time, negatively impressed Clausewitz, and helped drive the views of this very independent mind in a contrary direction. Trust in inventive strategy—"the play of chance and probability within which the creative spirit is free to roam"—and suspicion of any tendency towards the doctrinaire are basic to his thinking.[7]

Other examples of the context at work are provided by Clausewitz's identification and definition of some of the permanent elements he posited as existing in war. These basic elements are of different kinds. They range from the characteristics, as he sees them, of specific actions—for example, that attacks weaken as they progress, a concept that may have lost some of its validity with the rise of modern military technology, or that a major victory brings about many small successes—to the relation of theory to practice, which, as we know, he declared should be that of a guide not of a law. He sought to expand his analytic view of war by including on the one hand the relationship of organized violence to policy and politics, and, on the other, the realities in the field that accompany the transformation of strategic decisions into operational and tactical action: unplanned events, misunderstandings, accidents—whether happy or fatal—and errors of all kinds. No one needs to be told that in war as in life the expected and intended are easily interrupted; but Clausewitz lifted this common knowledge out of a general, often insufficiently consequential awareness, gave a name to unforeseen obstacles in war, and identified "Friction" as a permanent element that an analysis of war as such and of any war in particular needed to incorporate.

Creating a formulation that identifies and summarizes a major characteristic of war, in the process giving it a name that is more than an arbitrary label but already indicates its content, is of potential value to an all-embracing theory, and such formulations, which pinpoint the element in question, are an inherent part of *On War*. Clausewitz identifies another of these basic components with his characterization of war as the continuation of politics or policy by other means. Again a generally known, if often inadequately understood fact—that war has a political purpose, determined by the holders of executive power in a political entity, whether a highly centralized state, a loosely organized tribe, or an interest group within the larger society, and that the conduct of war also has political consequences, some of which are linked to its purpose while others are not—is concentrated in a few words, and as Clausewitz shows that these words may affect and be affected by every other component of war, the statement turns into an element of great analytic force, particularly powerful because it is sufficiently elastic to accommodate conflicts ranging from wars between states to civil and irregular wars of all kinds, and accommodates as well the possibility of changing the political end in the course of fighting.

Friction and the interaction of war and policy are two very different yet basic properties of war. Another element, the significance of which Clausewitz never ceases to stress, is that of the psychology of the combatants, including the issue of morale and attitude of the troops, but also attitudes of the population, the society that wages war, and the psychological make-up of supreme commanders and officers in charge of units of some operational autonomy, or on detached missions. Under the influence of his teacher Scharnhorst, Clausewitz began to emphasize this point as a student in the Institute in the Military Sciences for Young Infantry and Cavalry Officers and in his earliest historical writings, from which he transferred it to his theories, a path from history to theory taken by many of his fundamental ideas and recognitions.[8] He never doubted that psychic forces could overwhelm the cleverest rules of action— which themselves often were the result of emotion as much as of impersonal calculations. But here we encounter a limitation of the times in which he wrote. The relevant theories and literature of the eighteenth and early nineteenth centuries did not offer him the structured hypotheses with which to analyze the significance of both an individual's psychology and the feelings and emotions of groups, a social or political elite, inhabitants of a particular area, or "the people." Instead he had to rely on such works as the nearly one-thousand-page-long descriptive catalogue of human traits by the psychologist Friedrich August Carus, well received in the early years of the nineteenth century and republished in 1823, a work that Clausewitz might well have consulted when he was writing *On War* but that lacked any central analytic theory of the development and interaction of these traits. In the absence of such a theory—and he himself refers to "our slight scientific knowledge," which does not allow him "to go farther into that obscure field"—his long chapter on "Military Genius" in *On War* is an unending search from one concrete personality trait or type of behavior to another for an unidentified central dynamic that brings them together.[9] The scientific and cultural context in which Clausewitz writes lacked the generalizing, integrating psychological system he would have found useful.

Finally, the impact of the times in which he wrote is again noticeable in his treatment of one of the central theoretical building blocks of *On War*. At the conclusion of the work's revised first chapter, after Clausewitz reiterates that wars differ "with the nature of their motives and of the situations that give rise to them," he returns to their degree of sameness, the basic uniformity of all wars: "Its dominant tendencies always make war a remarkable trinity—composed of primordial violence, hatred, and enmity, which are to be regarded as a blind natural force; of the play of chance and probability within which the creative spirit is free to roam; and of its element of subordination, as an instrument of policy, which makes it subject to reason alone [*der untergeordneten Natur eines politischen Werkzeuges, wodurch er dem blossen Verstande anheimfällt*]."[10] Clearly this last characterization does not reflect reality; it expresses a wish. Clausewitz hopes that war as a political tool remains in the hand of pure and practical reason. Still, having reduced the variety of forces acting and interacting in war to three ever-present "dominant tendencies" is a great achievement. In its universality it strengthens both the analysis of war as such, it also contributes to the understanding of particular situations—for one, it rejects thinking, speaking, and planning of a "purely military decision or action." But Clausewitz goes further, and in the following paragraph attaches each of the three abstractions—violence, chance, and subordination to reason—to a concrete agent:

> The first of these three aspects *mainly* [my emphasis] concerns the people; the second the commander and his army; the third the government. The passions that are to be kindled in war must already be inherent in the people; the scope which the play of courage and talent will enjoy in the realm of probability and chance depends on the particular character of the commander and the quality of the army; but the political aims are the business of government alone. These three tendencies are like

three different codes of law, deep-rooted in their subject and yet variable in their relationship to one another. A theory that ignores any one of them or seeks to fix an arbitrary relationship between them would conflict with reality to such an extent that for this reason alone it would be totally useless.

These words strike a further blow at theorists of war, who are at once prescriptive and exclude all but narrowly defined military considerations from their teaching.[11]

To lend his trinity the concreteness and specificity that he always seeks so as to give substance to abstractions, Clausewitz attaches the three basic aspects or characteristics of war—one of which, the subjection of policy to reason, expresses a rational conclusion that in the real world can be no more than a wish—to three definable agents in historical and current reality—the people, the army and its commander, and the government. But even with Clausewitz's reservation that the links he posits are not exclusive, his pairings obviously lack the universality, marred only by the final wish or expression of hope, of the first trinity. For one, the "passions that are to be kindled," which need not be limited to "primordial violence," and which Clausewitz assigns to the people, may exist elsewhere as well—in the army, and particularly in the political leadership, where a readiness to employ violence tends to have stronger and more far-reaching results than a similar willingness of the population at large. In Frederick the Great's Silesian Wars, conflicts that Clausewitz traced and analyzed in what are among his clearest and most profound historical works, the initial decision to go to war and then to continue fighting rested first with Frederick, and after he had invaded Silesia with the Habsburg Empire, which decided to resist the invasion, and fight to regain its province. It is unlikely that the ordinary Silesian burgher and peasant felt hatred either of Berlin or of Vienna, except after experiencing invasion and occupation, and in a society as regimented as that of eighteenth-century Prussia, the feelings of the mass of the population hardly counted, aside from loyalty and the habit of subordination. Equally, Napoleon's pursuit of policies that led to the violent deaths of hundreds of thousands far outpaced the effects of any popular hatred or aggression. "Primordial violence," broadly diffused through segments of the population, did play a role in the French Revolution; but even the Terror was instigated by individuals and small groups, not by the population at large, and apart from the uprisings in the Vendée and the Tyrol, as well as phases in the protracted conflict in Spain, the enraged people can hardly be said to have had as significant an impact on the course of events as did Napoleon and his crowned opponents and their advisers in starting and waging the wars of the French Revolution, followed by the wars of the French Empire. To repeat, emotions leading to or supporting violence as an active historical force, which Clausewitz assigned primarily to the people, were in fact or potentially also present and active in the other two components of the trinity. His desire to emphasize the link of each abstract component of his triad with a particular historical entity—the people, the government, the army and its commander—seems to have pushed him to conclusions that he knew could not be taken literally and that moreover he himself rejected in his historical writings and his political views.

Very likely the already-mentioned absence of sufficiently comprehensive psychological theories that met his needs in finding appropriate links for the three bases of his trinity contributed to these conclusions; certainly they were also influenced by events of the time and the impact they had on him. For the young man's intellectual and emotional development, the French Revolution was a major experience, disturbing but eventually liberating in its demonstration of the temporary nature of many of the beliefs and doctrines in which he was brought up. When decades later he came to associate violence with the people, he was undoubtedly thinking of the French Revolution, to be precise recalling how as a boy and then as an ensign he heard of episodes of popular violence in France, and remembering his exposure to the ideological statements of both the revolutionary government and its opponents in France and abroad. For the mature Clausewitz now to write that the passions needed in war must already be present in the people, is in fact a recollection of experienced history and an expression of his political views that originated in the 1790s: people should not be inert subjects but informed and feeling citizens, not a passive but an active force as at times they were in France. As we know from his political essays and correspondence, so far as the Prussian state is concerned, he is not yet thinking of broad and direct political participation, but of greater local self-government, the expansion of regional representative bodies, and a responsible ministry—the ideas of 1788, all political and social changes that for the Prussian state in the early decades of the nineteenth century were highly contentious and their realization still far in the future. The trinity expresses Clausewitz's political wishes: the people should be engaged, just as policy should be determined by reason. Historical experience, political wishes, and a desire to shorten the distance between theory and reality here result in smudging the clarity without, however, reducing the analytic value of his profoundly enlightening tripartite conception of war.

Although some of the forces that shaped Clausewitz's second trinity can be identified, not every intention and motive that went into its formulation is known. The reader of the concluding paragraphs of the opening chapter of *On War* is left with a text that at first sight seems confusing, and one that contradicts any number of the author's other statements. Such complexities are, of course, common hurdles of textual interpretation. Here, if a complete explanation may be unattainable, the available facts nevertheless take us far. Above all, the second trinity merely amplifies the first; the basic truth of the tripartite characterization of the nature of war is never compromised. Comparing the statements in the second trinity with Clausewitz's biography and with a multitude of Clausewitz's writings beyond *On War* reveals that the associations he posits do not represent his considered opinion. For a few seconds we hear the French Revolution speaking to the young ensign, a voice to which he responded strongly then and throughout his life. In today's debates on the trinity, confusion and error could be avoided if the historical influence on Clausewitz's phrasing of his second trinity as it elaborates the first, and links abstraction to historical reality, were taken into account.

Clausewitz's trinity, the questions raised by the second trinity, and their suggested resolution as sketched out in the preceding paragraphs illustrate the impact that events in Clausewitz's life and times could have on the sense and wording of his theories—an impact that, far from strange and unusual, is of course in the order of things and to be expected. The three brief paragraphs on the trinity in *On War*, its sentences resting on the young man and future author hearing and reading of the events in revolutionary France, are one example among many of the direct relevance Clausewitz's life and experiences had on his work. The trinity and one of its elements—humanity's readiness for violence, interacting with the army's management of violence, and the government's use of violence to achieve political goals, all of which to greater or lesser extent are touched if not suffused by psychological motives—show us that the two paths that lead to Clausewitz, text and context, not only approach each other and often intersect, but for a time may even develop and move forward as one, in this case biography shaping theory, even down to the words that help give the idea permanence.

Such correlations challenge the historian, and for good reason; but they cannot be expected to excite those of Clausewitz's readers today who are primarily interested in aspects of war in their time. Too often they read *On War* as a work intended to be a definitive guide, which may or may not have something valid to say today. Others, more in accord with Clausewitz's intentions, read the work as an aid to their independent thinking. Still, it is not difficult to see that Clausewitz's purpose is to lay bare and understand the components of war and their interactions, a part of that understanding being that doctrine can go only so far, and that it is derived from people, ideas, and events that define the time in which the author lived. The man who, Marie von Clausewitz wrote, "first showed him the right course," his teacher Scharnhorst, and with nearly the same immediacy Kant in his critique of the logical observation of reality that Clausewitz encountered as a student—did not tell him what to think. [12] Instead Scharnhorst and Kant, each in his own way a major voice in German thought of the time, freed his mind, and lent it tools with which to become productive: the nonprescriptive study of history, which gave Clausewitz the sense of change that allowed him to take hold of the present, and a way of observing reality that enabled him to turn action into abstraction—tools developed at the time and in the spirit of the culture in which he lived and wrote.

When later readers study and weigh the significance of his work, part of their determination should rest on the understanding that Clausewitz's ideas are expressed in terms of the years in which they were written, and do not always readily translate into equivalents today. Just as the Constitution of the United States contains ideas that should be read with an understanding of the social, technical, and cultural differences between then and now, so *On War* expresses realities that, without altering their essence, must be adjusted to conform to the passage of time, and that deserve not the literal but the creative reception that the work's author asked and hoped for.

Notes

1. "Context" is here used not with any of the specifically military meanings that the recent literature sometimes attaches to the word—e.g. context as an operative concept in the theory of war—see, for instance, Thomas Waldman, *War, Clausewitz and the Trinity,* 45–46, 55–57, etc.—but rather in the word's general sense of environment, which includes but goes beyond background.
2. For the bases of his analytic method, see the second essay, 22–26.
3. A review of H.D. von Bülow's *Lehrsätze des neuern Krieges*. See the second essay in this volume, fn. 26.
4. The title of a section in Book 2, ch. 2 of *On War,* 141. In a preceding section, entitled "A Positive Doctrine is Unattainable," Clausewitz has already stated that "it is simply not possible to construct a model for the art of war that can serve as scaffolding on which the commander can rely for support at any time" (140), yet he evidently feels it necessary to make this point more than once: "[Theory] is meant to educate the mind of the future commander, or, more accurately, to guide him in his self-education, not to accompany him to the battlefield; just as a wise teacher guides and stimulates a young man's intellectual development, but is careful not to lead him by the hand for the rest of his life.," etc. (141).
5. Ibid., 61.
6. A recent example, Derek Leebaert, *To Dare to Conquer,* Boston, 2007, 10.
7. Clausewitz, *On War,* Book 1, ch. 1, 89.
8. Note the discussions in the second essay in this volume, pp. 22–23, of Clausewitz's answer to a test, and in the third essay in this volume, pp. 79–80, of the analysis of Gustavus Adolphus in his early study of the Thirty Years' War.
9. Clausewitz, *On War,* Book I, ch. 3, 106.
10. Ibid., 89.
11. Ibid. On the Trinity see also the fourth essay in this work.
12. Marie von Clausewitz, "Preface," ibid., 65.

2

A Learned Officer among Others

In 1801, Lieutenant Clausewitz of the 34th Infantry Regiment, having acquired the necessary approval from his commanding officer, applied for admission to the Institute in the Military Sciences for Young Infantry and Cavalry Officers in Berlin, and was accepted. The Institute, founded by Frederick the Great, schooled promising junior officers selected from regiments throughout the army, who attended the Institute for three years in autumn and winter, and returned to their regiments in spring and summer. For the school's administration and classes a single room in the royal palace had been set aside, signaling both high approbation of its task and characteristic Prussian parsimony in carrying it out. In the year Clausewitz was admitted, the Institute, in recent times not highly thought of in the army, was provisionally placed under the charge of Lieutenant-Colonel Gerhard von Scharnhorst, a Hanoverian officer who had just transferred to the Prussian service. Among his various new duties Scharnhorst was soon made permanent head of the school, for which he developed a new curriculum and chose new instructors to join two faculty members who remained from the previous era, a veteran major of Engineers and Professor Johann Gottfried Kiesewetter, a well-known teacher of Kantian philosophy, who lectured on mathematics and logic. Scharnhorst himself taught strategy and tactics, and also gave talks on military history and on the duties of the General Staff.[1] As though to convey to the service he had just joined that not only junior officers needed encouragement to think about war, he helped found and headed a study group, the Military Society, of officers and government officials, some of senior rank, others junior or in mid-career, who read and discussed papers, which were published in the Society's *Proceedings*. The institute and the society, guided by the same outsider, began to raise the intellectual sophistication of a generation of Prussian officers, who came to maturity in the defeats suffered in the War of 1806, and contributed to the victories gained less than a decade later. For Clausewitz, attendance at the institute, but particularly the bond he formed with Scharnhorst, inspired his thinking about war and largely shaped his career.

The new head of the institute differed in his modest social antecedents from the typical Prussian field-grade officer. Still, he possessed qualifications that in these years made him a person of interest to the king and his advisors. Frederick William III, only recently ascended to the throne, and the officers on whose opinions he relied, were anything but determined innovators, yet Prussia's recent campaigns in France and against insurgency in Poland convinced even them that some matters needed to be changed: not only the structure of the army, which lacked permanent units beyond the regiment, but also its central administration, as well as the limited educational institutions for officers that then existed. A soldier from another state, tested in combat, a writer on a wide range of military topics and an experienced educator, appeared to them a potentially useful advisor in their cautious efforts to adjust the monarchy's army to the changing military circumstances of the day.

The son of a Hanoverian noncommissioned officer whose family owned a small farm, Scharnhorst had served in the Hanoverian army since 1778, taught in its new artillery school, and formed close contacts with professors at the University of Göttingen, whose empiricism he integrated in his own thinking on how to approach war and its many issues objectively and logically. By the outbreak of the revolutionary wars he had become known beyond Hanover as an editor of military journals, a writer on military institutions and on the history of the more recent European wars, and as an author of technical works on gunnery and of such more encompassing military works as the three-volume *Handbook for Officers on the Practical Parts of the Military Sciences,* published between 1787 and 1790, and the *Military Pocketbook for Use on Campaign,* a volume of 517 pages in octavo, published in 1792, a work that contained basic instruction for officers in charge of small detachments, on the "little war" of outposts, patrols, ambushes, raids, the construction of entrenchments, and the attack and defense of fortified places.[2] The work became a contemporary classic, was reprinted three times and translated into English; buyers often had it bound in leather, with empty pages for notes, to carry in a saddlebag or backpack. In the campaign of 1794 in the low countries Scharnhorst distinguished himself in combat and as an ad hoc staff officer, was repeatedly promoted, and rose to the rank of Lieutenant-Colonel. In 1797 after peace returned, he published, as an introduction to a series of articles on the campaign of 1794, a long essay on "the general sources of the French successes in the revolutionary war," an incisive analysis, which in its realistic, nonideological approach to the interaction of military, political, and social innovations that made the Republic's conduct of war so effective, towers over other early studies of the changes in warfare ushered in by the French Revolution.[3]

Scharnhorst's awareness that in Hanover promotion to the rank of Colonel or above for the son of a noncommissioned officer was close to impossible made him receptive to suggestions he might consider service elsewhere, and the Prussian officers who opened negotiations with him in 1799 were not troubled by his service in the army of another state. That he had no ties to factions or institutions in Prussia could even be seen as an advantage, and certainly was no impediment. Throughout the eighteenth century, as the Prussian monarchy expanded, the army regularly filled its rank-and-file with foreigners, German and non-German, and recruited promising officers from other forces throughout Europe.[4] In 1801, following an extensive correspondence and several meetings with Prussian representatives, and offered substantial inducements, including a title of hereditary nobility he requested for the sake of his son's future in the new country as much as for his own, Scharnhorst resigned from the Hanoverian Army and changed into Prussian uniform.

In his interests and career, Scharnhorst personified and by his example advanced a social and intellectual development that in the last decades before the French Revolution began to make itself felt in the standing armies of continental Europe. Even in the Hanoverian service, in which a noble title, buttressed by suitable family circumstances and connections, were weighty factors in receiving a commission and subsequent promotion, members of the middle classes formed a significant proportion of officers in the artillery and engineers. In Prussia, after the experience of the Seven Years' War showed the need for specialists in reconnaissance, raids, and security, light forces became more numerous and it was not as difficult for sons of middle-class families to be commissioned in these new formations, leaving the heavy infantry and cavalry to continue observing the traditional values. Over time this differentiation between the social characteristics of the various branches in the Prussian service became difficult to maintain at the formerly expected degree of purity, the granting of titles of nobility accompanying and facilitating the introduction of middle-class officers—subalterns as well as officers of higher rank—in line units, the expanding central staff and administrative sections, occasionally in the guards.

Even as Scharnhorst's position, first in the Hanoverian, now in the Prussian Army, represents a more general trend, his career and his many writings also identify him as a special type of officer often associated with this social development: the "learned officer"—the German *gelehrter Offizier* perhaps implying a greater affinity with the academy than would the English equivalent. The term was used both as a neutral designation of an officer possessing special knowledge in fields ranging from mathematics and technical matters to the humanities, or as a polite alternative to the derisive noun *Federfuchser* [pen pusher], referring to an unsoldierly middle-class scribbler in uniform. In the Prussian Army the denigrating implications of the term were reined in by the fact that the monarch who in three wars had raised Prussia from regional significance to that of a European power could be considered the intellectual in uniform above all others. Everyone knew that Frederick the Great, not only the head of state, but an intensely active and creative strategist and field commander, showed similar, even equal energy in scholarly and cultural matters. He wrote as much on political theory and history as on military affairs, to say nothing of his musical compositions, countless poems, and the vast correspondence he maintained with philosophers and scientists throughout Europe. With his snuff-stained uniform and deplorable posture on horseback, the king even seemed to confirm and at the same time soften the potentially comic or socially demeaning attributes often attached to the term "learned officer."

Scharnhorst's casual posture, head bent forward, unlike the upright tautness customary in the regiments of the Berlin garrison, did at first occasion disapproving comments. The newcomer's bearing was compared to that of a professor in uniform, and stressing his academic character became so widespread that years later it made its way even to Napoleon's secret service, an informant referring to Scharnhorst as "*ancien professeur de Goettingen, homme savant.*"[5] After his death this mode of seeing and depicting the peculiar quality of his personality and intelligence entered the iconography of the Prussian state. It is evident not least in Christian Daniel Rauch's 1822 statue of Scharnhorst that today stands in the square before the Berlin Staatsoper. In the sculptor's conception of the reflective man of action, the figure's fully achieved realization of German classicism already humanized and brought from Apollonian heights to earth by touches of a romantic sensibility, the statue is if not of a piece with, then closely related to, Rauch's well-known sculptural portraits of Goethe.

By the time Scharnhorst left Hanover for Prussia, the learned officer had come to reflect not only a social development, but also a cultural change. Even beyond its social make-up, organization, and doctrine, the Prussian Army of 1800 was no longer the army of three generations earlier. Several writers and even a poet or two had served in the wars of the mid-century; now the officer corps included a fair number of men to whom the arts, especially literature, meant more than the few poems they had been drilled to memorize as cadets. The high and late Enlightenment—in Prussia driven not least by Frederick's example—had reached beyond small intellectual elites, so that some general familiarity with recent and current literary works, even the wish to write oneself, was now a widely accepted and expected fact of existence in the middle and upper classes. This development was to mark Clausewitz's entire life, and thus his work. We know from his recollections that he believed literature played a decisive role in his intellectual development when in adolescence he began to break out of an ensign's narrowly defined service routine. Even his earliest surviving writings show an awareness of style and precision; he wrote poetry occasionally—if not above the common standard—and literary references and allusions punctuated his work and his daily existence. When the twenty-one-year-old entered the Institute for Young Officers and came under Scharnhorst's influence, these tendencies and abilities were ready to be directed towards the analysis of matters of professional concern in a mind that was expanding from the military into the social and political sphere, and beyond that to cultural forces and trends.

Scharnhorst's reports and writings together with some surviving notes and exercise books of his students convey a fairly good sense of the way instruction proceeded at the Institute. Just as Scharnhorst did not address the reality of war from a doctrinal perspective, he did not teach the prevailing Prussian doctrine by rote. No doubt the school's lectures and assignments constantly referred to the nature and components of the tactical and operational systems then followed, but these systems were not at the center of instruction. Instead Scharnhorst emphasized specific problems, and how they could be examined, understood, and dealt with within the limits of what in the Prussian service might be acceptable. Thirty years later, in an essay on Scharnhorst that was as much the author's intellectual biography as a defense of his admired teacher against conservative critics, Clausewitz was to write that Scharnhorst "taught that part of the art of war that until then had scarcely been dealt with on the lecture platform and in books—war as it basically and actually is [*der eigentliche Krieg*]."[6] What Clausewitz meant with these words is illustrated on the small-unit tactical level by a short assignment to the students that has survived from 1803, together with Clausewitz's answer, the "Solution to the 26th Assignment."[7]

The assignment, closely related to the tactical discussions in the first chapter of Scharnhorst's *Military Pocketbook,* asks the student to explain how the Berlin garrison can with certainty determine that the enemy has occupied two positions at what was then the city's edge. Clausewitz responds in four paragraphs, in which he details the formation of two patrols, outlines their missions, and traces the routes they are to take: Two sneak patrols [*Schleich-patrouillen*], led by noncommissioned officers, are sent out; one consisting of three foot soldiers, the other of three foot soldiers and three mounted men. Clausewitz adds an explanation for including men on horseback in the second patrol: "The cavalry serves in part to bring rapid reports, ... and in part because the men on foot will consider them as support, and will advance with greater courage. They will not feel as abandoned [*sich so verlassen fühlen*]." He concludes, "If the patrols do not return, it is very likely that the enemy has occupied the two positions. The men are not to carry packs, and if possible should be given dark overalls [in place of the standard white infantry britches]. They are promised a monetary reward."

In its few lines, Clausewitz's answer to the 26th Assignment encompasses the whole awfulness of war. Men are sent on a mission. If they do not return they may be assumed to have fulfilled it. Aside from taking this central conclusion for granted, his answer raises two further issues for the later reader, one merely of an organizational nature: should a patrol that intends to stay hidden include men on horseback? Presumably at the time the area in which the assignment was set consisted of fields, woods, and villages, with people working in small farms and moving on the roads, among whom horsemen might not stand out. But whether or not the inclusion of mounted men suited the particular situation, the second reason Clausewitz gives for adding them to the patrol makes his answer historically significant. Even in the freer atmosphere that spread through the army after Frederick's death, when officers no longer faced the possibility that any step beyond the commanded and customary might expose them to the king's wrath, few would have justified adding cavalry to the patrol with the explanation that horsemen would raise the musketeers' sense of security. The tactical and disciplinary concepts according to which the army functioned would have made a serious discussion of this issue unlikely, perhaps impossible. As long as the core principle of Prussian tactics consisted in infantry in a firefight marching in columns and firing in linear formations, and cavalry attacking in compact squadrons, the paramount function of the individual musketeer or cuirassier was to act in unison with the mass, a duty that could not be questioned. That in his answer Clausewitz mentioned the feelings of the rank-and-file in combat in a nonderogatory manner, and did not hesitate to note what might be done to allay their fears, conveys a sense of the questioning, realistic nature of Scharnhorst's instruction, which reached beyond regulations to help the student confront the realities on the ground and in people's minds.

Beyond revealing something of Scharnhorst's method of instruction, Clausewitz's response to the 26th Assignment is his earliest known statement related to the development of his ideas, apart from some recollections of his feelings as an ensign at the end of the Rhine campaign of 1795, to which he referred in a letter to his wife many years later. His answer documents the origin of one of his important, even basic thoughts on war. Together with passages in his first historical studies, written at the same time or very soon afterwards, the answer to the 26th Assignment is an early indication of two linked elements that became permanent in his thinking: his suspicion, soon coalescing into absolute rejection, of universal rules, fixed responses in strategy and operations, a denial he often extended to tactics as well, an attitude grounded in his sense of the uncertainty and unpredictability of war; and secondly the significance he attaches to one of war's great uncertainties, the psychic characteristics and feelings of the men engaged in it—whether heads of state and generals, or company commanders and common soldiers—a significance going far beyond the usual consideration of "morale." In his solution to the 26th assignment Clausewitz connects psychological factors directly to military practice on a basic level, as in his early history of the Thirty Years' War he links them on the highest plane by identifying the psychological characteristics of King Gustavus Adolphus as the key to Swedish strategy. The attention Clausewitz gives to the feelings of the individual in combat is documented again some years later in his lectures on the little war, in which he goes so far as to point to the *positive* consequences of fear when fighting individually rather than in the mass.[8]

Clausewitz's sensitivity to psychological factors in his historical and theoretical work must have originated in childhood tendencies that developed further as he grew up.[9] But the attention he paid to people's feelings and how emotion influenced their actions was also encouraged and influenced by statements and opinions he encountered as an adult. Important among these are passages he found in Scharnhorst's writings. To give one example, in the already mentioned essays on the Campaign of 1794, published four years before Clausewitz became his student, Scharnhorst includes an editorial note with the following remarkable comment: "The psychological part of the art of war is ... a subject that is not at all well understood. It is for this reason that the principal benefit to be derived from history, acquiring the difficult and yet so useful knowledge of the human heart, an understanding most easily achieved by studying events resulting from vast and far-reaching intentions, is almost completely lost."[10]

Scharnhorst's emphasis on *intentions* is interesting. He would not have wanted to deny history the task to record overt facts; but by stressing the intentions that led to the facts, for example the decision to go to war or the choice of a particular operational objective, he points to issues that are too easily pushed aside with generalities. If, however, Scharnhorst's words "the principal benefit to be derived from history" are meant to apply not to readers of history in general, but to those who study history to gain a better understanding of war, it can at least be argued that he might have thought that being able to trace a sequence of strategic or operational events was less useful than to know the opponents' intentions and the issues and ideas that gave rise to them.

Aside from the impact on their analyses of war of Scharnhorst's and Clausewitz's interest in psychology as a hard-to-comprehend but significant key to its understanding, it is worth noting that subsequently these ideas did not fully disappear in Prusso-German military thought. Several generations after Scharnhorst published his introductory essay on the successes of the French revolutionary armies, the editor of his military writings commented on the passage quoted above with words that move from historical interpretation to express a current conviction:

These lines clearly identify Scharnhorst's views of the writing of history … To summarize them briefly, he regards a history of what was wanted and planned [*eine Geschichte des Gewollten und Gedachten*] as more important than a history of actual events, events that depend so much on the accidental and fortuitous. In the study of history it is certainly more instructive to trace the inner *causes* of events than the events themselves, and to pay particular attention to the psychological forces, which play such a major role in war.[11]

This comment gains substance from the fact that its author, the future Field Marshal Colmar von der Goltz, was anything but a theorist remote from the realities of the service. Born in 1843, and at the time of editing Scharnhorst's writings a Lieutenant-Colonel on the General Staff, von der Goltz was the author of two important works on modern war and a history of the Prussian Army from 1757 to 1806, *Von Rossbach bis Jena*—that is, from a remarkable victory to a stunning defeat—a documentary analysis that, even if von der Goltz lacked Clausewitz's passion for objectivity, is among the early works in German military history that extensively uses material dealing with social and intellectual conditions as well as with sources on military and political events. Between 1883 and 1896 von der Goltz was detached to the Turkish Army, which he did his best to modernize on the German model. After returning to Germany he served as chief of the army's Engineer and Pioneer Corps, and was seen as a possible successor to Schlieffen as chief of the General Staff. In the First World War von der Goltz commanded the 6th Turkish Army in Mesopotamia, blocking all efforts to relieve the British force at Kut-el-Amara, which in April 1916, two days after his sudden death, led to the surrender of 10,000 British and Indian troops. To von der Goltz as to Scharnhorst and his pupil Clausewitz it was self-evident that both the rational conduct of war and the interpretation of war in the past demanded paying attention to the irrational.

In the history of Clausewitz's efforts to study war objectively and comprehensibly, the "Solution to the 26th Assignment" documents his early rejection of the absolute authority of doctrine and rules. He knows their value, understands that they constitute a great and necessary advance over untaught armed action, are essential in matters ranging from making and breaking camp to close-order tactics; but he also notes their limitations and—especially in the spheres of strategy and operations—their self-destructive potential in accustoming men to carry over the belief in rules and doctrine to areas that demand flexibility and independent judgment. The recognition of the importance of one's own and the enemy's emotions and the ease with which these convert into customs and principles is joined to an understanding of the flaws and dangers inherent in systems of rules and practices that brook no opposition. These two recognitions further combine with a widely known fact and its less easily grasped implications: the components making up the reality of combat—attack, defense, envelopment, etc.—are affected by the specifics and uncertainties of each situation, which in turn are influenced by the attitudes and ideas of the individuals engaged in it—all elements that require doctrinal mastery, and yet may demand more than a response by rote—as do operational decisions and strategic plans.

Clausewitz had entered the Institute towards the end of 1801, and Scharnhorst quickly recognized and responded to his ability and promise. Soon teacher and student developed a close attachment. In later years Clausewitz was to refer to Scharnhorst as a second father, "the father of my spirit," elevating the not uncommon bond between student and teacher to heights of familial intensity. Already in March 1802, Scharnhorst included an essay by Clausewitz in a group of student papers he thought deserving to be submitted to Frederick William. In a report to the king of 1803 he went further and divided his students into four groups according to their degree of "ability, judgment, industry, and knowledge."[12] The highest-ranking group consisted of Clausewitz and another student who had entered the Institute the same year, but had been promoted to lieutenant a year before Clausewitz, Carl Ludwig Heinrich von Tiedemann. Years later, the future field-marshal and minister of war Hermann von Boyen was to call Tiedemann the best educated officer in the army. A third student in that class, Johann Jakob Rühle von Lilienstern, was placed in the next highest group. Both Tiedemann and Rühle were to be a presence in Clausewitz's life from then on.

Clausewitz's relations and correspondence with the people closest to him—his wife, Scharnhorst, and later Gneisenau, who did his best to protect and guide his younger friend through the social and political vicissitudes of a military career—have been extensively discussed in biographies and histories, and in editions of the works of Clausewitz and of his contemporaries. We know far less of the many other relationships Clausewitz formed in the course of a richly faceted life, and there is still much to explore in the social and professional context in which he served and wrote. The recent appearance of numerous letters of Marie von Clausewitz to her husband indicates that further documents or other information on his life may yet be recovered, a promising source besides his wife and one or two close friends being individuals who at one time or another and sometimes over decades were in contact with Clausewitz, without over the past two centuries attracting much attention from his biographers. To pay overdue notice to such persons in his environment, and to see him from a different, more inclusive perspective, broadens the linear, factual sequence of his life. In an earlier attempt to pursue the conditions and relationships that come into focus as the biographical lens is widened, I considered Clausewitz's career in conjunction with one of his contemporaries, Heinrich von Kleist, who entered the Prussian Army at the same time as Clausewitz, but then left the service, eventually to write dramas and prose works that made him one of the great figures of German literature.[13] The contrasting and joint overview revealed a number of similarities in the concerns of the two men—one a dramatist, the other a historian and theorist—and suggested affinities between some of their reactions and even of the conclusions they reached in their works that could be worth pursuing.

It seems useful to take up this comparative view again, but now expand it and trace Clausewitz's life from his years at the Institute for Young Infantry and Cavalry Officers together with and against the lives of several of the men he came to know or know of at the time. To see Clausewitz not by himself as an autonomous thinker, but to follow him from the years when he was a promising young officer interacting with comrades and superiors, and compare him with others making their way in the same demanding organization at the center of a complex and changing society during years of major international crises and military challenges, should give us a better sense of Clausewitz's life, and of the matrix of events, feelings, and ideas in which it was lived. It may also tell us something further about elements of his thought as they were formed and expressed in response to events and conditions of his time, in agreement with or in opposition to the attitudes, ideas, and actions of his contemporaries. We know the large lines of his life; additional details, incidental or significant, are revealed when the perspective is enlarged to view him together with a number of contemporaries who share his experiences in the Prussian Army in peace and war, and are concerned with the interpretation in theory, history, or literature of some of the same issues that Clausewitz was beginning to think about. If this means taking an interest in men who until now figured only marginally or not at all in his biography, it does not lead us away from him. On the contrary, seeing Clausewitz jointly with his peers gives us not only a fuller sense of his world, it points to so far unrecognized facts and ideas that bear directly on his thought.

In selecting men with whom to compare him, and link or contrast his ideas with theirs, it makes sense to turn again to Heinrich von Kleist, his exceptionally gifted and distinguished contemporary, who grew up in the Prussian Army in the same years as Clausewitz, and add two already mentioned promising students at the Institute for Young Officers, Tiedemann and Rühle von Lilienstern, the latter an intimate friend of Kleist, together with another close friend of Kleist and also of Rühle, the broadly gifted young Guards officer Ernst Adolf Heinrich von Pfuel. All were of the same generation as Clausewitz; five young lieutenants, whose abilities and interests seemed to be turning them into "learned officers."

• • •

Kleist and Tiedemann, the oldest of the men here considered with Clausewitz and he with them, were born in 1777, three years before Clausewitz. Tiedemann, the son and nephew of generals, came from a family of officials and officers.[14] Kleist, son of a captain, later major in a Prussian infantry regiment, belonged to an impoverished branch of an old, prominent family; during Heinrich von Kleist's life more than fifty officers of his name served in the Prussian Army.[15] Like Kleist, Pfuel, one year Clausewitz's senior, bore one of the monarchy's oldest names; the Pfuels are already documented in the thirteenth century.[16] His father, a lieutenant-colonel, had married without requesting the obligatory royal permission, which if the bride, as in this case, was the daughter of a company surgeon, a man whose position in the service placed him somewhere between a sergeant and an ensign, Frederick the Great would have been unlikely to grant. In consequence of the bride's socially inappropriate father, the king, though he had a high opinion of Pfuel, demanded he leave the service. After his wife's early death, Pfuel returned to the army, and Frederick appointed him to the potentially influential position of chamberlain in charge of the court of his nephew and successor, the later Frederick William II, who on his ascension to the throne promoted his chamberlain to the rank of major-general, and made him head of a section in the Supreme War Council—a sequence of events in the life of one officer that exemplifies the Prussian nobility's powerful yet porous position in the state at the end of the eighteenth century, the high significance of class distinctions from which nobles benefitted, and the monarch's easy manipulation of these differences.

The distinction and prominence over centuries of the Kleists and the Pfuels could not be matched by the ancestors of their common friend, Rühle, who was born in April 1780, six weeks before Clausewitz.[17] Nevertheless the Rühles, as the Tiedemanns and the others, were a known and respected family. The father, a retired lieutenant, lived on his estate and served as counsel of the regional association of nobles. All four families, in spite of their different histories and current situations, were firmly situated at the core of the monarchy's military elite, a social entity at the edge of which the Clausewitzs maintained a precarious foothold. Clausewitz's father, son of a professor of theology, following family tradition considered and referred to himself as noble, and served as a lieutenant in a Prussian infantry regiment, from which he was forced to resign when he could not document his noble descent. That subsequently Clausewitz and two of his brothers rose to the rank of general was made possible by their grandmother's second marriage to a Mecklenburg noble and Prussian colonel, whose family and rank vouched for the standing of his new grandsons. Clausewitz's career is an example of the gradual influx at the end of the eighteenth century of men of the middle class and even—as in the case of Scharnhorst—of well-to-do free peasants into the officer corps, an ascent often facilitated by ennobling the newcomer, or by the common, unofficial acceptance of a claimed title, which once its bearer attained significant rank was legally acknowledged, as was to be the case with Clausewitz and his brothers.

The regiment Clausewitz entered through his step-grandfather's influence was a unit of some social distinction, its ceremonial chief being Frederick the Great's youngest brother, Prince Ferdinand. The commanding officer when Clausewitz joined the regiment was Colonel Ernst Friedrich von Rüchel, an intelligent, arch-conservative officer, a stickler for regulations, who had been won over by the system builders, and believed that the "undisciplined" armies of the French Revolution could be outmaneuvered, immobilized, and smashed by the application of mathematically precise combinations of movements. Scharnhorst described him as "full of energy, but, to be sure, overly relying on the petty tactical arts."[18] His inability in emergencies to depart from the manual was to contribute to the army's defeat at Jena in 1806. Evidently this martinet left a lasting and negative impression on the young Lance-Corporal Clausewitz, who more than thirty years later, in a characterization that became famous, depicted his former commanding officer as being made up "of an acid of pure Prussianism," the personification of an unthinking traditionalism that quite inappropriately attached the name of Frederick the Great to all that was methodical and conventional in the Prussian service, a royal mark meant to make blind obedience inviolable.[19]

That the 34th regiment was nominally headed by a royal prince granted its officers some measure of contact with the royal court, a slight, but potentially important link that contributed to Clausewitz's first appointment after leaving the Institute as well as to his acquaintance with a lady-in-waiting of the Queen Mother, Countess Marie von Brühl, his future wife. Kleist had no need of such fortuitous institutional connections. Though three years older than Clausewitz, and privately educated until he was fourteen, he entered the army as a lance-corporal in the Footguards in the same year as Clausewitz, 1792, at the beginning of the war with France. The guards and the 34th Infantry Regiment fought in the same campaign and in some of the same battles, which makes it most likely that the two men knew each other then or later; that they knew of each other is certain, even if it cannot be documented.

In 1795, after the Footguards returned to Potsdam, Rühle joined the regiment as an ensign. Pfuel, holding the same rank, came to the regiment two years later. Neither man had yet seen action. They quickly became friends, soon including Kleist in what grew into an intense relationship that continued over many years. The three young officers were drawn to each other by common interests in literature, philosophy, and music. Rühle played the bassoon, and for a time he, Kleist on the clarinet, and two other officers formed a quartet. One summer, bored with their largely military circle of acquaintances in Potsdam, they decided to cross the Harz Mountains as wandering musicians, playing for their supper in farms and villages—at once the exuberant act of young men, perhaps also an expression of rebellion, above all a statement of the early Romantic delight in the power of unaffected emotion and in the idealization of simple humanity, unschooled men and women who were beginning to personify both nature and natural feelings to educated society, sentiments that reached their cultural and aesthetic peak in the words and melodies of the German *Lied*. A further bond linking Pfuel and Rühle was their acquaintance with Rahel Levin, a central figure in the small community of cultured, assimilated Jews in Berlin, to whom they were introduced by Pfuel's friend, the young lieutenant Varnhagen von Ense, Rahel's future husband. Their association was to last beyond the Napoleonic era. Pfuel, as will be shown, never lost the progressive bent of his youth, and in Rahel's diaries and letters his name appears many dozens of times.

The intellectual and cultural preoccupations of the three friends influenced their political views. Under the pressure of French expansion they were exchanging the Prussian, even Brandenburg particularism of their parents for a wider German consciousness, which saw German history and culture as a force that demanded greater political cohesion among the many states in which Germany was divided. These ideas are also evident in the thinking of the young Clausewitz, who in one of his early essays writes about the French advance across the Rhine not in patriotic phrases, but by trying to understand the dynamic of French political and military regeneration and comparing it to German passivity. The occupation of German territory he sees as a deplorable act that must be reversed, but also as a natural consequence of France's new power. "France," he writes, "cannot be reproached for setting her foot on our land, and for spreading her realm of timid vassals to the Arctic Ocean." Instead, seeing both sides of the issue, he holds the political fragmentation of Germany into dozens of states and principalities responsible. To retain their independence from the powerful neighbor to the west demanded a greater measure of political cohesion, even at the cost of limiting the autonomy of the particular states. It was an early sign of Clausewitz thinking of the German states and territories not only as cultural but in some respects also as a political entity, ideas that in 1812 helped drive him from Prussia. Serving the immediate interests of the Prussian state was coming to mean less to him than defeating Napoleon for the broader German and European good, as he saw it.[20]

Beyond the political views of the young men, their distaste of the discipline and narrow social tone they found in the Guards further strengthened their friendship, and soon led them to question whether they should remain in the army at all. Kleist, already driven by exceptional ambition and phantasies of unique achievement, called his time in the service "lost years." That in 1798 he addressed a memorandum to the newly crowned Frederick William III, criticizing Prussian infantry tactics as behind the times, a missive he then did not send, suggests that it was not the army as such he found objectionable, but the rigidity of the post-Frederician system, an authoritarian-administrative network that hampered the army and weighed on society as a whole. In

Kleist's mind it may also have stood for a world that did not welcome and allow the full unfolding of his genius. The following year, despite opposition from his superiors and his family, he managed to obtain absolute leave so that he could devote himself "to the higher theology, to mathematics, philosophy, and physics."[21] Pfuel, too, after a related request for leave to study in Paris was rejected, asked to be allowed to resign his commission, a wish the king eventually granted.

Rühle might have followed his friends, had his application in 1801 to the new Institute for Young Officers not been successful. He was admitted to the first class of students the same year as Clausewitz. Intelligent and energetic, Rühle early on also displayed social gifts. According to one contemporary he was among the most agreeable and pleasant officers of the Potsdam garrison.[22] A part of his response to a question concerning patrols, similar to the 26th Assignment answered by Clausewitz, has survived, and documents his high urbanity. "It needs no more than a glance," he writes in the introduction to his answer,

> to realize that my essay is not only my first of this kind, but that until now I must have lacked any occasion to see patrols and read orders pertaining to them. It will therefore be particularly pleasant for me to be instructed not only on this point, but on everything that might be demanded of or assigned to a patrol of the stated strength. Matters, on which, lacking any experience, I am hardly able to have clear opinions at all.[23]

According to his anonymous biographer cited earlier, at the Institute Rühle was particularly influenced by Professor Kiesewetter's lectures, "which brilliantly combined mathematics, philosophy, and the natural sciences," and laid the basis, the author notes somewhat ironically, for Rühle's "determination to find a guide for his entire existence in an intellectual attitude that above all sought contentment in life by abstracting its phenomena."[24] From the same lectures, Clausewitz by contrast acquired not only a general sense of Kant's reasoning, but in particular became acquainted with Kant's analysis of the fundamental elements of the scientific method as applied to society and its practices, ideas that are beginning to be reflected in essays and notes Clausewitz wrote before 1806, and that continued to influence him throughout life. It may also have been from Kiesewetter's lectures that Clausewitz learned of Kant's declaration that independence of judgment was an ethical imperative, unless he had already encountered the idea in Kant's widely known essay of 1795, addressed to the general educated reader, *What Is Enlightenment?*

That Clausewitz read the essay is not documented, though in view of its appearance in a prominent, nonacademic journal it seems likely that he did. Nor, beyond notes of Kiesewetter's students, including notes by Clausewitz, do we possess the text of Kiesewetter's lectures; but Kiesewetter may well have mentioned Kant's ethical teachings, and he certainly outlined Kant's critique of knowledge, which in its specificity on the nature of judgment and scientific interpretation would have given a young man attempting to find his way in the study of war much to think about. Briefly, Kant declares that because pragmatic experience is necessarily expressed with a priori concepts and judgments, it is an inadequate basis for a general system of knowledge. Empirical laws are no more than generalized particular experiences. They can always be denied by contrary experience. Observation and thought—and thought includes intuition—are the sources of understanding. But a priori assumptions may be contained in each. Since they compromise true understanding they must be recognized and isolated, which becomes possible by thinking beyond the limits of experience.

Although Clausewitz's program of studies included Kant's writings, and he subsequently read the works of other systematic thinkers, he was anything but a trained philosopher. But in his efforts to abstract reality he evidently welcomed the guidance he received from Kant by way of Kiesewetter. Is it too far a speculative leap to suggest that having learned that a priori conditions endangered clarity and objectivity, he attempted to overcome them by developing a nonjudgmental recognition of the nature of war, its causes, and its functions? He certainly followed Kant in studying both the phenomenon of war as a whole and its components in detail. In his critique of the scientific method, Kant writes that the scientist (or theorist) must recognize both the specificity of phenomena and their commonality, the relationship that links different phenomena. In turn, Clausewitz hoped to achieve a level of understanding that rises above personal experience and the study of the past, however necessary both may be. In its intellectual foundation, the manner of thinking that led Clausewitz to *On War* and to the work's exploratory rather than dogmatic message reflects these aspects of Kant's teaching.[25]

...

In 1803, Clausewitz, Tiedemann, and Rühle left the Institute. With Scharnhorst's backing they were given appointments that took them out of regimental service. Tiedemann became an "officer of the army," a title held by a small number of officers of all ranks not attached to a particular unit or office. Clausewitz was made adjutant of Prince August, nephew of the king, a young man who felt that members of the royal family should consider military service as more than a ceremonial obligation, and who would be an influential figure in the army in years to come. Rühle was attached to the staff of the quartermaster general, then transferred to the general staff and assigned to Prince Hohenlohe's army corps. He soon became a protégé of the corps' chief of staff, Colonel von Massenbach, a proponent of strategy as an exact, predictive science, whose failure in October 1806 to liberate himself from the manual and counter the speed with which the French advance interfered with the Prussian Army's development around and beyond Jena was to contribute to the defeats of Jena and Auerstedt. For Rühle and Clausewitz their appointments were the first in a succession of staff and special duties that extended largely unbroken through the rest of their careers. During the following years, Rühle and his two friends, Pfuel and Kleist, who had resigned their commissions, at times lived and traveled together, and when apart carried on an intense correspondence. Pfuel soon regretted leaving the army, and in 1805 was able to return as a second lieutenant, now not in the Guards but in a light-infantry battalion. Kleist continued his restless, driven existence, moving from place to place, as the struggle to express himself in dramas and prose works, accompanied by doubts whether and how he could combine literature with a military or civil position, began to resolve itself into the bursts of creativity on the highest level that marked his life from then on. He read and wrote incessantly, but remained an engaged observer of political and military developments. At the end of 1805 he accurately predicted to Rühle that Napoleon would soon attack and defeat Prussia. "Yes, dear Rühle," he wrote, "what is to be done? Apparently the times want to bring about a new order ... Is there no-one who will fire a bullet through the head of this evil spirit?"[26]

In these years, the last of the old monarchy, Clausewitz's attention shifted from reading and writing history to the theory of war. In paragraphs and short essays not intended for publication he began to develop his ideas on the relationship between war and policy; the earliest that have survived date from 1803 and 1804.[27] Closely linked to these notes was his first publication, a review of Heinrich von Bülow's *Doctrine of the New War*.[28] In essence, the review confronts Bülow's abstractions with Scharnhorst's realism. The twenty-four-year-old lieutenant not only rejects Bülow's operational theories as unduly mechanical, and thus unrealistic in conflicts between antagonists who are free to set their own rules, but he also questions the assumptions behind such declarations as "advancing along correct lines greatly lessens the importance of combat." It is inconceivable," he writes, "how intelligent people could have reached the opinion that strategy lessens the value of tactics, ... [and] that a further development [*Ausbildung*] of strategy means depriving combat of much of its decisive role."[29]

Underlying Clausewitz's critique is his denial of the late-Enlightenment idea that a "scientific" conduct of war could eliminate much of its violence—the point is important enough for him to repeat in the opening chapter of *On War*—an idea that minimizes and even ignores the variety and uncertainty of war, the constantly changing reality on the ground, and the psychological components of war, which range from man's fundamental willingness to maim and kill to the character, personality, and ability of the opposing commanders, including the effects that their independent judgments may have. Worth noting as well is Clausewitz's manner in rejecting Bülow's arguments—his language is unusually harsh for a discussion of this kind, and veers into the personal. His aggressive tone may reflect the author's inexperience; it also signals his undiplomatic frankness, a trait he only gradually brought under control.

Kleist, who had briefly held a position in the Prussian financial and commercial administration, resigned from it in July 1806, and was an unemployed civilian when war broke out in September. The other four young officers served in the fall campaign. During the retreat after the Battles of Jena and Auerstedt, fought on the same day some fifteen miles apart, Clausewitz as adjutant of Prince August, Rühle on the staff of Prince Hohenlohe, and Pfuel as adjutant of Lt. General von Schmettau, became prisoners when their units surrendered. Rühle and Pfuel were soon released, but Clausewitz was compelled to accompany Prince August to imprisonment in France and from there to Switzerland, not to return to Berlin, still occupied by the French, until November 1807. Tiedemann had a more successful war. First on temporary duty with the General Staff, he was assigned to the corps of General Kaminski in the spring of 1807 when Russia entered the war, and became known for his cool operational sense. Both Clausewitz and Rühle wrote and published reports of the lost campaign: Rühle a short book, soon reprinted, in which he loyally defended the mistaken decisions of Massenbach under whom he had served. Scharnhorst called the work "even more miserable than the miseries it describes";[30] Clausewitz still in the winter of 1806 a series of articles, a detached, objective account of the military events, published in the first months of 1807.[31] He does not hesitate to point out strategic and operational errors on the Prussian side, but merely hints at basic systemic failures, the institutional elements—administrative and political as much as military—he was to turn into the central theme of the personal, very critical history of the same campaign he wrote in the 1820s. Clausewitz's two publications, one written as a junior adjutant, the other as a general some twenty years later, exemplify the process of early appearance and subsequent development of important themes that frequently marks his work.

Prince August and Clausewitz were compelled to wait in Berlin until March 1808 before the French authorities permitted them to travel to East Prussia, where the king and the rump Prussian government were located, and Scharnhorst now headed the commission charged with reorganizing the remnants of the army that Napoleon allowed the much reduced Prussian state to retain. Scharnhorst soon separated Clausewitz from his duties with the prince, and made him head of his office. For the next years, Clausewitz, promoted to captain, and in 1810 to major and member of the new General Staff, served as Scharnhorst's close assistant. For some months he also acted as military tutor of the fifteen-year-old crown prince and two other, even younger princes. During the Second World War, a time particularly pressed to find simple solutions to complex issues, an English translation of the draft of his lessons, *The Most Important Principles of War,* gained unjustified authority as an introduction or even summary of Clausewitz's mature theories.[32] An outline of lessons addressed to young men who had not yet experienced war, delivered years before Clausewitz began to write *On War,* hardly deserved that measure of attention. Still, the notes contain expressions of Clausewitz's thinking at this time on such matters as the relationship of theory to reality, the reality of "friction" as a constant presence in war, and the significance of what might be summarized as men's psychological readiness and maturity to think and function in combat, particularly men of superior rank and responsibility. More important for the creation of a new army than these tutorials were the duties Scharnhorst assigned to Clausewitz, among them membership on the committee that drafted the regulations for the infantry, a new, more flexible, less formalistic system of infantry tactics and operations to replace the outdated system that ten years earlier Kleist had condemned in his memorial to Frederick William III, which in the end he did not send.[33] This and other assignments placed Clausewitz near the center of the military and political efforts to develop and implement the expansive reform program, duties that were to occupy him until the beginning of 1812. Tiedemann's career followed a similar route. Since he had one year's seniority over Clausewitz, had escaped capture and distinguished himself in the spring of 1807, he not only reached the rank of major earlier, but was also made head of the study commission of the new War Academy in which he and Clausewitz became the first instructors, Clausewitz lecturing on the "Little War," Tiedemann on tactics and strategy. As late as 1820 Tiedemann's lectures were thought to have sufficient lasting value to be printed for the army's internal use.

Clausewitz's lectures at the academy had two functions: one was to acquaint future battalion and regimental commanders with the purpose and methods of patrols, outposts, and ambushes, and show them the importance of combining such actions with those of larger units that moved and fought in dense formations—something that except for a few mechanical drills of the fusilier battalions had never been taught in the army. Their second aim was indirect but equally significant: to influence the student's general thinking about combat and war by liberating them from their customary reliance on actions of a largely inert mass of men responding mechanically to the orders of their superiors. Passive adherence to tactical doctrine might or might not be appropriate in a particular situation, but it could also color one's thinking about larger operational and strategic issues, about war itself. Clausewitz's lectures, given a decade after he had been a student, reflect Scharnhorst's conceptual linking of tactics and strategy in rejecting the artificiality of "scientific" strategic doctrines that at the time were formulated with a new intensity in response to the unexpected, "irregular" actions of the armies of the French Republic.

In contrast to Clausewitz and Tiedemann, both of whom remained in the much reduced army, and as Scharnhorst's assistants were engaged in developing the military reforms for which Kleist had called in the years before the war, Pfuel and Rühle had no part in the reforms and in the political conflicts fought over their adoption. In January 1807, shortly after being released from captivity, Pfuel, accompanied by Kleist, went to Berlin, then still under French occupation, where, as former Prussian officers without apparent occupation, they were arrested. Pfuel regained his freedom without much difficulty, but Kleist was taken to France and imprisoned for six months until his unworldly harmlessness was established. He returned to Germany, where Pfuel and Rühle tried to help him make a new life for himself. In the course of the army's demobilization after the lost war, both men had left the service, and sought new positions. Rühle married in 1808, the year he was appointed governor of Prince Bernhard of Saxe-Weimar, second son of the Grand Duke, the patron and friend of Goethe. On his recommendation Pfuel was taken on as an additional teacher. As Pfuel had a strong interest in sports, which he believed should be an important part of military training, he also became the prince's fencing instructor. Their posts gave the two friends official standing and a presence in Weimar, then a center of German literary culture, Rühle combining his supervision of the Weimar prince with intense literary activity. He was full of ideas, and expressed them easily in smooth prose, which up to a point obscured his tendency towards the complex and verbose. Over the next years he completed an amazing number of books and articles on a variety of subjects. In 1808 he published his first nonmilitary work, *Hieroglyphs or Glances from the Realm of Science at the History of the Day*, in which he constructed a mathematical concept of visualizing and studying history by means of maps, drawings, and graphs, going so far as to depict the history of the world in the form of a cylinder, based on the surface of the earth, its height indicating the passage of time.[34] He also launched a military journal, *Pallas*, subtitled *Journal for the Art of Politics and the Art of War*, that he edited and published from 1808 to 1810, and to which he contributed historical studies as well as strategic and operational essays that opposed the "geometric and geographic" concepts of war promoted by Bülow. In their place Rühle developed his own, particular view of war, an odd combination of the realistic and the romantic—not so much defining what war was as declaring what it ought to be: pragmatic actions for high purposes, and thus one of the noble arts.[35] The essays contained early expressions of ideas that, fully matured, were to determine his critique of Clausewitz's *On War* in the 1830s.

Possibly influenced by Rühle, Kleist decided to start a journal himself, and in January 1808 joined with a new acquaintance, Adam Müller, a well-known, early-romantic political philosopher and much published author, to bring out a new periodical, *Phöbus: A Journal for the Arts*, which Pfuel and Rühle helped finance. The first issue of *Phöbus,* on its cover an engraving of Apollo guiding the four horses of his chariot through the heavens, contained essays on literature and the arts by Kleist and other authors, as well as fragments of one of Kleist's dramas. He introduced the issue with a rhymed "Prologue," which, referring to the engraving of Apollo, opened:

> Thunder ahead, you with your fire-limbed horses,
> Onward through unending space, Phoebus, bring forth the day! [36]

If Kleist does not quite identify himself with Apollo, poetry personified, the prologue at least depicts him as the God's close follower: a poet conscious of his powers, shedding light as he overcomes all obstacles, whose visions and rhymes mankind will in the end acknowledge and praise—the verse specifically mentions an earthly observer as the God flies overhead. Kleist was to resort to the motif of the poet soaring through space once more, in his last drama, *Prince Frederick of Homburg.* The repetition suggests how greatly the vision of flying above and beyond the world captivated him, a phantasy born from his vast ambition, battered by unending disappointments and failures, that nevertheless continued to drive him forward, and yet was to fall far short of his posthumous triumph.

With its broadly based interest in forms of modernity *Phöbus* was well received; but although its seriousness attracted attention and approval, the journal lasted little more than a year. Financial reserves were inadequate, and that Goethe with his towering cultural presence took a view of Kleist's work that at best was ambivalent may have contributed to the journal's demise—for Kleist yet another defeat. Goethe did not deny Kleist's ability; he even staged his serious comedy of crime masquerading as justice, *The Broken Jug,* in the Weimar court theater. A success in Weimar would have given Kleist the literary stature for which he longed; but bad luck intervened. For a time during the rehearsals, Goethe worked with an early version of the text, rather than with Kleist's more effective revision. That he directed the play without much sympathy for the dramatic universality of what on the face of it seemed a harmless peasant comedy centering on a burlesque trial in which the judge, upholder of the law, was the criminal—a characteristic Kleistian dichotomy—contributed to the failure, after which Kleist damaged himself further by choosing to express his disappointment with vulgarly insulting Goethe.[37] Yet even under better circumstances the expectations the two men had of their art and of themselves would have been difficult to reconcile. Goethe was not averse to using themes of conflict to reach balance and sublime harmony; but he shared neither Kleist's fascination with violence nor his belief that contradiction and conflict provide the key for unsparingly direct representations of reality. In an important essay Hans Joachim Kreutzer has noted that "hardly any of Kleist's works manage without war," and it is this orientation to some form of conflict that brings his works of drama and fiction into a surprisingly close relationship to Clausewitz's historical and theoretical writings.[38] Natural disasters or conflicts, ranging from a lawsuit or a duel to wars of conquest or annihilation, strife between individuals and within the individual are always the cause or background of the event Kleist chooses as his subject, and usually form the substance or much of the event itself.

It characterizes this psychological and moral interpenetration of opposing forces that Kleist could begin the first paragraph of his novel *Michael Kohlhaas* with the sentence, "On the banks of the Havel, around the middle of the sixteenth century, lived a horse dealer, named Michael Kohlhaas, a schoolmaster's son, one of the most honest and most terrible men of his time"—words that receive their programmatic explanation in the paragraph's closing sentence: "It was his sense of justice that made him a robber and murderer."[39] The novel, based on a story Kleist heard from Pfuel, of an honest man who is cheated by a noble, cannot find justice in a world dominated by sloth and self-interest, and reacts with a campaign of violence and terror that expands into civil war in the center of Germany, is paradigmatic of Kleist's sensitivity to and acceptance of the powerful coexistence of seemingly contradictory emotions in the individual. That he sets his story in Reformation Germany, soon to be torn by religious wars, further strengthens the link he always draws between conflicts within the individual and conflicts in society and wars between states, which in his calm acceptance of even the most extreme events he presents as merely reflecting the strengths and limitations of men and women.

After *Phöbus* was discontinued early in 1809, Kleist went to Bohemia, attracted like other Prussian officers, active or retired, by the war that had broken out between Austria and France. There he met Pfuel again, who after marrying in the spring of 1808, left Weimar and had seen action in Bohemia and Saxony in one of the free corps of men from various German states organized to support the Austrian Army. Another volunteer recalls Kleist and a friend in the common room of an inn playing the *Kriegsspiel*, a popular military game that Pfuel developed further as a tool for understanding war by coding the elements of purpose, means, chance, and will, and tracing their interactions. A Prussian officer, Colonel von dem Knesebeck, offended that these young men continued to play in his presence and unable to accept the representation of war in a board game, even for analytic purposes, repeatedly told them that the game lacked this or that essential part of real war. To each objection Kleist responded, "But dear Knesebeck, it is all there." When finally the colonel asked how the game dealt with the issue of supply, and Kleist once again assured him that even the matter of supply could be included in the players' thinking and planning, the colonel shouted at Kleist to go to the devil and left the room. Knesebeck, a determined opponent of Scharnhorst's reforms even as he presented himself as forward looking and innovative, was a man of influence in the conservative circle around the king, whose senior adjutant he became in 1813. In the last weeks of Clausewitz's life Knesebeck was to be his immediate and intensely disliked superior.[40]

Kleist wrote verses to express and inspire German opposition to Napoleon. One of these, the poem *Germania to Her Children*, mirrors and responds to *Allons, enfants de la patrie!*, the chant, defensive in purpose, but aggressive by nature, that memorably gave voice to the forces that since 1789 were bringing military defeat and political upheaval to the German states. In Kleist's poem the chorus shouts,

> My brothers listen!
> Through the darkest night
> Descends a thunderous call:
> Germania will you rise?
> Has vengeance come?[41]

To Kleist and his friends it was obvious that since no one German state, nor even the Habsburg Empire, could halt French expansion, a closer combination, temporary or permanent, of all German states had become essential. That was also Clausewitz's conviction, a belief he would not repress when Napoleon in the fall of 1811 compelled the Prussian government to take part in the impending invasion of Russia. In February 1812 Clausewitz was to explain why he could no longer server in the Prussian Army in his *Memorial of Confession*, the emotional language of the document echoing Kleist's tone in *Germania to Her Children*. In his wish to make his writing meaningful to the present, Kleist, encouraged by Pfuel, proposed to start a new political journal *Germania*, to help inspire an all-German resistance to Napoleon. The Austrian authorities seemed disposed to support Kleist's plans, but the French occupation of Vienna, followed by the Peace of Schönbrunn in October 1809, put an end to this project as well.

While Pfuel and Kleist served with the Austrian forces, Rühle, now a Weimar colonel, and his charge Prince Bernhard found themselves on the opposite side. As Saxe-Weimar belonged in the French orbit, the prince had to serve with the Saxon corps under Bernadotte, Rühle at the marshal's headquarters keeping the corps' operations journal. His acquaintance with Bernadotte was to benefit Rühle in 1813, when he served as a liaison officer between the various allied forces, while Bernadotte, having become crown prince of Sweden commanded an army against his former master Napoleon. Besides keeping the journal during the campaign of 1809, Rühle also wrote an extensive report on his experiences, couched as letters to a fictitious sister, published anonymously in 1810 and 1811 as *Voyage with the Army*, a work of 1,497 pages in three volumes.[42] Its unusual title, suggesting a traveler and observer accompanying a sizeable military force rather than a soldier on campaign, accurately reflects Rühle's attitude: he pays as much attention to the towns and countryside, the social and especially the cultural environment through which he passes, as he does to the strategic and operational decisions he records in the corps' journal, and to the engagements and battles he witnesses. Rühle's strong interests in the arts are signaled by the motto of the first volume, borrowed from Goethe's *Elective Affinities*—"We do not evade the world more surely than through the arts, and we do not connect with it more firmly than with the arts." Applied to war—art makes the unbearable bearable, as it exposes, explains, and often justifies war—the motto ironically turns into a truly Kleistian concept, reminiscent of the ideas, linking culture with armed action, that twelve years earlier Rühle had shared with Pfuel and Kleist as junior officers, and to which Kleist again gave voice in his short-lived journal *Phöbus*. The question whether war was an art or a science continued to occupy Rühle until he was satisfied that war was an art, possessing—and that may have been what he principally wanted to assert—all the ethical prerogatives inherent in art. The claim eventually led Clausewitz to write a succinct, important discussion of the subject in *On War*, in which, without naming Rühle, he demolished the argument.[43]

The first volume of Rühle's *Voyage with the Army* has a frontispiece of an architectural drawing and a view of Dresden, and its first hundred pages mainly discuss German art and architecture, notably landscapes by Caspar David Friedrich. Rühle does not integrate his two subjects, art and war, but deals with them side by side. It is not until the seventh "letter" that he turns to the diplomatic prelude and military preparations of the campaign. His analyses are what might be expected from an intelligent and reasonably well-informed observer; more striking are his observations of the military reality: how soldiers individually and in the mass function as they move from peace to war, on the march, singing, in bivouac, preparing for combat. Rühle's close descriptions of men on campaign, an example being his account of French surgeons after the Battle of Wagram operating on three large tables, while wounded men in line wait their turn, are strong examples of the literary realism that classicism could accommodate without losing its formal balance.[44]

Napoleon's victory over Austria, his second in five years, seemed to confirm the stability of his political restructuring of Europe. Yet the continued hostility of Great Britain, the war in Spain, uprisings in the Tyrol, and hit-and-run actions by small free corps in Germany kept resistance flickering and continued to agitate a military world not yet as divided along national lines as it was to become in the later nineteenth century. Rühle, Pfuel, even Kleist were prepared to move from service to service. Clausewitz, too, thought of leaving Prussia, but for the time being remained, as did Tiedemann; their commitment to Scharnhorst and their duties in the intermeshing reform agencies still holding them back. Rühle meanwhile left his position with Prince Bernhard, and for a time devoted himself to writing, while rejecting offers to enter Austrian, Russian, and even French service—this last an invitation, conveyed by Jomini, to join the headquarters of Marshal Ney, whose corps had been ordered to Spain.[45] In Dresden at the end of 1811 he announced public lectures on war as an element in human existence, which the impending invasion of Russia forced him to postpone. Pfuel entered the Austrian Army in 1810. Until given a regular assignment, he followed his interest in physical exercise and gymnastics by founding a swimming school in Prague, in which he taught soldiers the breaststroke, and organized exhibitions of up to two hundred swimmers. In November 1811 he was seconded to the War Archive in Vienna, where he studied the history of popular uprisings and drafted memoranda on military planning for officials and soldiers working towards new uprisings against the French. Kleist returned to Berlin, and in October 1810 launched a newspaper, the *Berliner Abendblätter,* which in its brief existence—publication ceased on 30 March 1811—printed a number of his short essays and anecdotes that are intellectual and stylistic masterpieces of German literature. Above all, he completed the drama on which he had worked since the second half of 1809, his last, *Prince Frederick of Homburg,* set in the reign of the Great Elector whose son became the first king of Prussia; the play's universal themes of obedience and free will carrying implications for the Germany of a later day. Kleist dedicated his play to Princess William of Prussia, a remote descendant of the Prince of Homburg and Frederick William III's sister-in-law, in the hope that the princess would accept the dedication, which would have gone far to assure the play's performance and success. Once again he gave himself up to unrealistic hopes; the drama's political themes and allusions and its psychological interpretation of the leading characters, which soared above the respect owed ancestors of the royal family, only confused and angered the king when he at last glanced at or was told of the text. A few days after Kleist sent the princess his manuscript he also wrote Frederick William, to volunteer his service in case of a new war with France, an honest statement but also an attempt to ingratiate himself, which generated no more than a few empty phrases in response.[46] As even Kleist began to recognize that no royal acknowledgment of his drama was forthcoming, that every effort to connect his life and creative energies to receptive individuals and institutions ended in failure, he gave up the struggle. He had recently met a married woman whose love of literature was driven to ecstatic heights by her awareness that she was suffering from a fatal disease. Within a few weeks she and Kleist concluded a suicide pact, and on 21 November 1811, at the edge of one of the lakes surrounding Berlin, Kleist shot his companion and himself.

• • •

It is not documented that Clausewitz ever read the text of *The Prince of Homburg* or saw it performed, although he might well have. That he knew of the work, its content, and how the royal family and Berlin society reacted to it is certain. The text was published in 1821, and after failed attempts to present it in Berlin and in Vienna, where Archduke Charles prohibited the play for its potentially demoralizing impact on officers and men of the Austrian Army, Marie von Clausewitz's cousin, Count Brühl, the director-general of the royal theaters in Berlin, arranged for the work's first performance in the Prussian capital on 30 July 1828, in a revised text that eliminated or obscured some of its most contentious passages. Even then the performance caused a small cultural scandal, and led Frederick William III to order "that the play must never be given again."[47]

What was it about *The Prince of Homburg* that kings and archdukes found so offensive?[48] The work, written when Prussia was a humbled dependency of France, certainly sounds a patriotic note. But besides evoking a heroic past, the play also contains elements that the current leading circles in state and army could find troublesome. Its plot is based on a battle fought in 1675 during the war Brandenburg and the Netherlands fought against France and its ally Sweden. On 18 June, near the Rhyn river by the town of Fehrbellin, northwest of Berlin, the elector with six thousand men encountered a somewhat larger Swedish force that had invaded Brandenburg from Pomerania. The Prince of Homburg, nephew by marriage of the elector, commanded the Brandenburg advance guard and was ordered to stay in contact with the enemy, giving the main body of the army time to deploy. Instead, he allowed his exploratory thrusts to expand into a general attack, which initially succeeded. But Swedish resistance grew, and it needed the main force under the elector to turn an increasingly difficult engagement into a decisive victory. The elector's order to prevent the Swedes from escaping across the river could not be carried out, and in his disappointment the elector threatened to have the prince court-martialed, but then relented. The battle, a step in the long political and military process by which the Electorate grew into the Kingdom of Prussia, quickly became a subject of legend, centered on the prince's initiative, which crossed the line into disobedience. Frederick the Great's account in his history of Brandenburg-Prussia, which Kleist appears to have read, is a characteristic version of the episode: "The Prince of Homburg abandoned himself to his fighting spirit and began an engagement that might have ended in disaster had not the elector, warned of the danger in which the prince found himself, hurried to his support. ... He forgave the Prince of Homburg for irresponsibly risking the future of the state, saying to him, 'Were I to judge you according to the harshness of the military code, you would have deserved to lose your life. But God does not want me to dim the brilliance of such a happy day by shedding the blood of a prince, who was one of the main instruments of my victory.'"[49]

Kleist takes a different view of the prince's actions and the thoughts and feelings that led to them. In the play's opening scenes, the evening before the battle, the prince, half asleep, sits in the garden of a small palace, the elector's temporary headquarters, and gives himself up to fantasies of glory, which he links with the image of a beautiful woman whom he eventually identifies as Natalie, the elector's niece. The play asks what sort of man is the prince, and begins to explore his feelings—a psychological enquiry that informs the work from beginning to end.[50] The senior officers assemble to receive their orders for the coming battle; the prince writes down the steps of the task he is given, but his twin visions continue to preoccupy him and he does not fully grasp the plan: he is to stay out of cannon range until one wing of the enemy is forced against the other. He will then push the disorganized Swedish troops into the swamps along the river. Instead he attacks early and with the elector's eventual help breaks through the enemy lines. The surviving Swedes flee across the river, leaving cannon and banners behind.

The lost battle causes the Swedes to propose an armistice. The elector nevertheless declares that whoever acted against the orders he issued deserves to be executed. When the prince presents him with three Swedish flags and reveals that he allowed his exploratory advance to turn into a premature attack, the elector orders him arrested. Homburg is certain that he will be quickly released, but the court-martial proceeds. Again he believes, "The elector has done what duty would demand; And now he will obey his heart as well."[51] Instead the court condemns him to death, and the elector signs the sentence. The news that the Swedish ambassador is negotiating a marriage between Natalie and a Swedish prince adds to Homburg's despair. He suspects the elector wants him out of the way for diplomatic reasons. His fantasies of glory and of love have betrayed him, and he now finds himself in extreme danger. On his way to ask the elector's wife and Natalie for help, he passes the grave that is being dug for him, and panics: "I saw my grave, and now want only life. And won't ask if it's glorious or not."[52]

His unrestrained fear shocks the two women; they promise to do what they can to save him, but Natalie also urges him to be brave. She appeals to the elector, who cannot believe that Homburg would beg for mercy, but promises, "If he can think the sentence is unjust, I'll take the judgment back and he is free."[53] He writes a note to that effect to the prince, and asks Natalie to take it to him, which she does, though she fears that Homburg will never agree to call the sentence unjust. She recognizes that the conflict between strict obedience and free will also has a personal side: The elector is more than the personification of a strict code of behavior. He, too, has emotions, among them pride in his position; he has strong family feelings for Natalie, but is also conscious of her potential as a prize in marriage diplomacy. The prince, on the other hand, is too easily pushed by his overbearing fantasies of glory to see himself in the elector's place. During the battle, as a rumor spreads that the elector has been killed, he cannot help himself and begins to talk and act as though he were now in command. The elector, who is not only alive but insists on the letter of the law, checks Homburg's ambitions, and the prince's self-image is shattered when he sees the open grave intended for him. Still, by the time he reads the note Natalie brings him, he has recovered his courage. Just as the elector, despite his insistence on obedience, is not blind to the value of initiative, so the prince recognizes the elector's belief in sensible rules, and his understanding that commands cannot be easily ignored combines with his search for glory to make him accept the sentence of death. He cannot be persuaded to call the judgment unjust, even when Natalie assures him that to do so is the only way he can save his life. Homburg's fear of execution has turned into a will to meet death—and it is difficult for the later reader not to see in this shift yet another instance of the author's identification with his leading character. Officers beg the elector to pardon the prince. An old colonel tells the elector that the highest law he should observe is not the letter of the law, but what benefits the country and the crown: "What do you care, I ask you, according to what rule the enemy is beaten, as long as he and all his banners sink before you? The rule that beats him is the highest rule."[54] The elector wants to know if the prince supports the officers' appeal, which Homburg denies. He merely asks that the elector grant him a last request, that Natalie's hand not be bartered for a peace with Sweden.

Homburg, blindfolded, is taken to the place of execution. As he waits for the firing squad, he expresses his feelings in words and images reminiscent of the prologue Kleist had written for the journal *Phöbus*, lines of verse that convert Homburg's impending death into the deathless glory he has longed for and that his victory in battle as well as his acceptance of the elector's sentence will bring him:

> Now immortality you are all mine!
> You shine, a thousand suns, into my blinded eyes.
> My shoulders become wings,
> I soar through still, ethereal spaces.
> As from a ship blown outward by the wind,
> We see the busy harbor disappear,
> So does my life fade in the gathering gloom.
> Colors and shapes I still discern,
> And then fog covers all.[55]

But the blindfold is taken from his eyes and the fog dissipates. The elector, who has succeeded in reasserting his absolute authority, crowns the prince with a wreath, and the assembled officers proclaim Homburg the victor of

Fehrbellin. He faints. As he comes to, he asks "Is it a dream?" To which the old colonel replies, "A dream, what else?"—one of the many transparent ambiguities that mark and strengthen the play. Has the drama ended happily—has individual initiative truly overcome passive obedience? A dream, what else? But for the moment Homburg's and Natalie's fate is resolved, and the play ends with the concerns of state and society again taking center stage, as the officers gathered around the elector and the prince shout, their voices combining sequentially: "To war! To war! To battle! To victory! Into the dust the enemies of Brandenburg!"[56]

For Kleist's drama to declare Homburg the victor over the Swedes amidst common jubilation and the eagerness to fight on for the glory of Brandenburg-Prussia may send the ironic, even subversive message that although the prince's attack would not have succeeded without the support of others, personal initiative may trump orders. The play's most immediately shocking incident, however, and one that had a particularly strong impact on Clausewitz's generation, is Homburg's panic as he sees the open grave in which he will be buried. Is that how a soldier, let alone a Prussian prince, reacts as he faces death! Homburg has suffered a psychic collapse, which he is unable to overcome during his meetings with the electress and Natalie. Other, less symbolically charged themes in the play are also startling, and more serious in their intimation not of human but of systemic weakness: Homburg's readiness to disobey orders and the officers' pleas for his life reveal that authority and subordination are not absolute—the pillar central to the army' structure and the elector's authority lacks the stability that is taken for granted. This message is emphasized by the colonel's blunt counsel to the elector. Not only does the old soldier give his ruler unasked-for advice, and comes close to implying that the army is organizing to support the prince; he twice rejects the sanctity and utility of unquestioned rules as such: an army is not an unthinking tool, he tells the elector, "like the sword lifelessly hanging from your golden belt." Frederick William III, and strict conservatives who opposed the more radical reforms of the Prussian Army after 1806 on ideological as well as military grounds, could only take the appearance on stage of a frightened German prince, as well as his autonomous actions, which the old colonel, who functions as the army's spokesman, defends by rejecting the finality of rules, as serious insults to the crown's authority.

The martial shouts at the end of the play bring together the contending factions, and there can be no doubt that with these exclamations Kleist "wanted to give a sign to his contemporaries."[57] His drama about the honored past emerged from Prussia's recent history, the military and political failure of an absolute monarchy, which, like the prince on seeing his grave, has fallen into seeming helplessness. And, as we know, the play is not the work of a detached critic. Not only is its tone informed by its author's seven years' service in the

Prussian Army, the condemnation by some of the play's characters of the inert obedience to rules—which carried a later, Kleist's, generation to disaster—echoes more comprehensively the poet's earlier criticisms of the army's tactics and discipline, which he planned to send the king in 1798, and which he repeats the following year in a letter to his former tutor explaining his reasons for having resigned his commission. The elector's readiness to punish the prince's disobedience by having him executed may even be Kleist's extreme symbolic exaggeration of the army's accepted practice of teaching the common soldier the complex maneuvers of close order drill, the core of Prussian infantry tactics, by having officers and drill sergeants beat them into conformity. Prussia's defeat in 1806 could only strengthen Kleist's long-held rejection of mechanical, quasi-scientific systems of war, and further assert his belief in the individual's intellectual and emotional capacities—in war as in literature. When he writes *The Prince of Homburg* a few years later, he gives these ideas dramatic form. As is true of many social interactions, war demands rules and their observance, but also the free play of creativity. Frederick the Great himself had made it clear that rules exist to be broken. During the Seven Years' War, hurrying his troops in forced marches to counter a crisis, he said of the units rushing forward without concern for alignment and properly buttoned uniforms, "my men look like grasshoppers, but they bite!" Fifty years later at Jena this understanding had been forgotten: care to march his men in deliberate step as near to the parade-ground model as possible kept a senior Prussian general, Ernst von Rüchel, the same who in earlier years was Lance-Corporal Clausewitz's commanding officer, from bringing his regiments forward in time.[58] That doctrine needed to be made flexible and space be created for individual initiative was the conviction of the determined reformers, whatever their political beliefs, from Scharnhorst and Gneisenau to Yorck and their younger assistants Clausewitz and Tiedemann, ideas and attitudes that determined their policies from tactics to discipline to operational conduct and strategic planning, and influenced some of them as well in their advocacy of a diminution of privilege in society, and a measure of wider participation in public affairs.

Kleist, coming from a different direction, confronts issues very similar to those that occupy Clausewitz in the same years, and reaches similar conclusions. Divested of its poetry, *The Prince of Homburg* reads like a case study of problems that Clausewitz's histories and theory address—the challenge of uncertainty in war, the extent to which doctrine and personal initiative can meet it; the impact of personalities on events, the significance of individual reactions to violence committed and suffered. In his classic study of Kleist's works, Friedrich Gundolf noted that in *The Prince of Homburg*, "hatred and combat are directly traced back to human qualities, and are discussed without reference to good and evil."[59] The same may be said about *On War*. The two works confirm each other's approach, and provide today's reader of *On*

War with powerful insights into Clausewitz's deepest concerns. Like Kleist, he seeks to understand the forces under discussion, an understanding that is easily compromised and diverted by—premature—moral judgments. The interest both men show in motives and reactions may also help explain how it is that they can feel free to ignore convention and talk about fear as one of the realities of war. In considering the impact of danger on the individual, as in the realization of the necessity to accept and carry out orders but also to rise above them, Clausewitz's perception of war waged between states and of the individual interacting with war as commander, planner, agent, or victim is in far greater sympathy with Kleist's views than with those of other military theorists of his time, the Bülows, Jominis, and Rühles.

Clausewitz, first in 1805 in his review of Bülow, from then on continuously in his theoretical writings, denies the validity of the schematic conduct of war, a rejection he first integrated in his early historical interpretations. Linked to his recognition that regulations are necessary in war, but that blind faith in them is unrealistic when it comes to make operational or strategic decisions— and often tactical decisions as well—is his awareness of the significance of feelings, emotions in all aspects of war, from the basic willingness to kill to make tactical and strategic decisions. A part of that understanding is his objective treatment of fear as a constant in war, something he first mentions in 1803 in his answer to the 26th Assignment, and raises again in his lectures on the little war, not as a reaction to condemn, but as a natural reality that should be taken account of, studied, and understood.

• • •

By the beginning of 1812, in the weeks after Kleist killed his companion in pain and committed suicide, the worsening international situation made evident that Prussia faced a major crisis: Napoleon was readying the French Empire and its satellites for a war to push Russia out of Europe, erect a firm Polish barrier in the east, and preserve and strengthen his Continental System. The German states now organized by France into the Confederation of the Rhine and the separate Prussian satellite were told the number of troops to contribute to the campaign, and administrative and communication centers and depots were established throughout central and eastern Germany to support the Grande Armée as it assembled and began to move east. Most officers of the small force that Prussia was allowed under the peace treaty with France accepted the situation, and followed orders. But some thirty, among them Clausewitz and Tiedemann, formally requested leave to resign their commissions, an act not only of legal force, but vastly symbolic in the autocratic Prussian state. Scharnhorst, when informed by Tiedemann that he was resigning, responded that "I cannot disapprove of your decision, because each of us must above all make certain to remain true to himself."[60] Publicity, let alone ostentatious declarations of sentiment or principle, were avoided; only Clausewitz used the occasion to explain his reasons and at the same time indict what he rejected as the suicidal selfishness of Prussian domestic and foreign policy. He wrote a *Memorial of Confession*—nearly seventy pages in print—had copies made, and sent one to Scharnhorst and another to his friend Gneisenau. He did not submit the *Memorial* to the king, who may nevertheless have seen segments of the text and certainly learned of the memorandum's content, which could only add to his displeasure at an officer who placed his personal views above the decisions of his king.

The document—part personal statement, part political analysis, part organizational and operational planning—begins by outlining Clausewitz's view of the feebleness and errors of Prussia's government and society, followed by two series of quasi-poetic declamations:

> I declare myself free from the frivolous hope for salvation by chance ...
> From the childish hope of exorcising the tyrant's anger by voluntary disarmament ...
> From the false resignation of a repressed mind.
> From the senseless lack of faith in our God-given strength ...

This declaration of independence from fear and passivity leads to a series of affirmations:

> I believe and affirm that a people has nothing greater to respect than the dignity and freedom of its existence.
> That it must defend these to the last drop of blood ...
> That the disgrace of a cowardly surrender can never be cleansed.

These "heartfelt effusions," as Clausewitz himself characterized them, are followed by a sober discussion of the political and military realities, and of the military means now available to Prussia, which, he emphasizes, include the possibility of organized popular uprisings.[61] In previous years units of retired soldiers and armed civilians began to be formed secretly throughout the state, and command and communication networks were organized for possible civilian actions to support the army in a new war. Clausewitz had taken part in these preparations. But they were never intended to trigger an uprising while French troops and troops of other states under French command moved through Prussia by the hundreds of thousands to the east—masses that pinpricks of irregular action would not have stopped, and could only have led to tighter French control. Nor was central and eastern Germany comparable to Spain, geographically or culturally. The inclusion of such phantasies in the *Memorial of Confession* represent one last outburst of the wish Clausewitz had stated more than a decade earlier, for a Germany that was not only culturally and historically one, but also politically more united, a wish he had first voiced in one or two of his earliest essays—the untitled study beginning *Whether the French Are Comparable to the Romans,* for example—in which he speaks of Prussia as a community of an armed patriotic people, a German version of revolutionary France, instead of the authoritarian state it was in reality, with politically inert subjects ruled by a monarch who continued to regard other German states as rivals and potential targets.[62] Now Clausewitz appeals to Frederick William III to broaden his political vision and place confidence in his people—a challenge the king would have found particularly offensive.

After 1812 the kind of emotional confessions and assertions at the core of the *Memorial* disappears from Clausewitz's political writings. He continues to criticize the inefficiency of the absolute monarchy in Prussia, supports a gradual move towards a more representative form of government, rejects the accusations of revolutionary plots with which Prussian conservatives countered every effort to broaden participation in public affairs; but his language grows more restrained as he concentrates on his historical and theoretical work.

In the second week of May 1812, while units of the Grande Armée were still moving to their assembly points, Clausewitz left Prussia for Vilna and the Tsar's headquarters, where he joined a growing number of German expatriates, among them Gneisenau. He soon received a staff appointment, the first of several, and added his voice to the debate over the appropriate strategy for countering the invasion; but since he knew no Russian and the international reach of the French language dissipated as the distance from headquarters increased, his appointments, whatever their official designation, were limited to those of advisor and observer. He rode with the main army as it withdrew to the interior, and after the Battle of Borodino with the rearguard to Moscow; from there he followed the army as Kutuzov turned southwest, flanking the French line of communications and bringing the long Russian retreat eastward to a halt. In September he learned that his friend and former colleague at the War Academy Tiedemann had been killed, news to which he reacted with tears, and that he was appointed to succeed him as chief of staff of the forces covering Riga. Since this could be nothing but another nominal position in an area that the French retreat was rapidly turning into a backwater, he decided to join the Russo-German Legion then being formed of German volunteers, and was appointed the corps' chief of staff. The Legion, the strength of which was to grow to 8,500 men, had greater political than military significance. It represented the commonality of Russian and German interests, even as Prussia and other German states were still allied with France.[63] Clausewitz had known several of the Legion's officers in earlier years, among them Pfuel, who after resigning from the Austrian service left Prague in July and made his way over Denmark and Sweden to Russia, where in September he entered the Legion as a captain. As time was needed to ready the Legion for action, Pfuel began to write a brief history of the invasion and its failure, continuing the account to December, and published it the following spring in liberated Berlin as *Retreat of the French*.[64] Clausewitz, impatient to be away from rear headquarters, asked to be temporarily assigned to one of the armies in the field, and in November was attached to Wittgenstein's corps, which was advancing towards the junction of the retreating main French Army with Macdonald's 10th corps withdrawing southwest from Riga.

By the middle of December Wittgenstein had moved between segments of the Grande Armée, his advance guard under General Diebitsch threatening to isolate the rear of Macdonald's corps, as its Prussian auxiliary force under General Yorck, still consisting of fourteen thousand men, was approaching the Prussian border. A temporary cease fire was agreed on, Clausewitz acting as intermediary in the negotiations that now began. Yorck, an active, innovative participant in the army's reforms, had no patience with Frederick William's hesitant policies. Clausewitz convinced him that his corps was in danger of being cut off, but could be preserved by being declared neutral, a noncombatant status the Russians would respect. Once Yorck had agreed, Clausewitz wrote the text of the document, named after the village where Yorck made his headquarters, some thirty-five miles northeast of Tilsit, the Convention of Tauroggen. Yorck's decision, reached without authorization from Berlin, was a late outcome of the message that both Kleist in *Germania to Her Children* and Clausewitz in his *Memorial* sought to convey: the defeat of Napoleon should matter more than the short-term interests and policies of the various German states. A further message the Convention sent was that under certain conditions orders could be disobeyed.[65]

The departure of the Prussian contingent, which had suffered far less than the forces retreating from Moscow, made it very difficult for Macdonald to attempt a stand on the Niemen. In turn the political consequence was to add pressure on Frederick William to separate his state from France. As the French retreat continued, Yorck, disregarding Berlin's order to resign, shifted from neutrality to overt support of the Russians. In East Prussia, now freed from French troops, the Estates met, agreed to support Yorck's corps, and voted to raise a militia for service outside the province and a home guard, according to a program drafted by Clausewitz, measures again undertaken without royal order or approval. These decisions further shifted the military balance, while compelling the king to remain in step with such privileged groups of his subjects as the East Prussian estates and turn against Napoleon, even as forward Russian units were pushing into Prussian territory. On 20 February mounted detachments of the Russo-German Legion, Pfuel one of their leaders, reached Berlin. After a few hours they withdrew, but their brief appearance signaled that larger forces were approaching from the east. On 28 February Russia and Prussia became allies; twelve days later the French garrison quit the capital, and on 16 March Prussia declared war on France.

Throughout 1812 Rühle had remained in Germany. As the French withdrawal continued, and the Prussian Army rapidly expanded, he returned to Prussian service, and was placed with the rank of major on the staff of the Prussian forces in Silesia under Blücher's command, with Gneisenau as chief of staff. In April Scharnhorst joined them. He had pushed rearmament forward, now he wanted to ensure that operations in the field were pursued with the energy that had been lacking in 1806. In Silesia Rühle after some years again met Clausewitz, who still wore Russian uniform, Scharnhost's and Gneisenau's request that Clausewitz be appointed to the General Staff having been denied by Frederick William, who prohibited Clausewitz's readmission to the Prussian Army until good conduct in the coming campaign had erased his error of leaving the army in the spring of 1812. In his place Knesebeck was appointed to the General Staff, the colonel who had argued with Kleist about the *Kriegsspiel,* and who on Scharnhorst's staff turned out to be as conventional as he had been when after 1806 he opposed meaningful innovations in the army's tactical and operational doctrine. Officially Clausewitz now served as a liaison officer; in reality he was again Scharnhorst's assistant until he needed to return to the Russo-German Legion.

Before leaving he wrote a brief account of the campaign of 1813 so far, a continuation of Pfuel's *Retreat of the French,* which in the following months was published and reprinted several times.[66] It was also at this time that Rühle assumed the task—whether he was ordered to do so or on his own suggestion is not clear—of updating Scharnhorst's *Pocketbook for Use in the Field.* Scharnhorst wanted a compressed version that would help the hundreds of new officers in the rapidly expanding army find their way through the practical demands of company and battalion duties on campaign. Instead Rühle, true to his nature, began to draft plans for a far longer work, which in the end he did not complete as originally planned. The finished parts finally appeared several years after the war.[67] In its new guise Scharnhorst's *Pocketbook,* originally a brief, practical manual widely used in German armies during the Revolutionary and Napoleonic Wars, expanded into a broad two-volume mixture of information and analysis, its facts and instruction enveloped in such extensive, often abstract discussions that the work proved of little practical value, and left hardly a mark on the military literature of the time.

In discussing Rühle's revision of Scharnhorst's book, his anonymous contemporary biographer regrets that the author, "who proved his worth brilliantly in the strategic sphere," limited himself when writing this work by covering only elementary topics, without discussing "the higher conduct of war," adding, "we can at least be pleased that with his work *On War* Clausewitz so neatly filled the gap Rühle left."[68] The praise of Rühle's strategic abilities refers, however, not to anything Rühle wrote or might have written on strategy, but to his service in the 1813 spring and fall campaigns. For both Napoleon and the Allies, the French failure in Russia had created great political and military uncertainties. Even after Prussia declared war on France in March, the Habsburg Empire remained neutral. Saxony, Bavaria, and other members of the Confederation of the Rhine had not broken with France, nor had Denmark, which depended on Napoleon's support in its conflict with Sweden over the possession of Norway. To detach the German states from the French Empire required at least the expulsion of French forces east of the Rhine. That, in turn, called for the Russian and Prussian armies to act in close agreement, a coordinated effort in an area from the Baltic to south-central Germany that at the time even closely integrated forces would have found challenging.

In some respects the situation the Allies faced at the beginning of 1813 was even more difficult than that of Napoleon: its members, driven by frequently conflicting political interests, pursued different strategies, and after Kutusov died in January were for a time without a commander-in-chief and an effective central staff. Under those conditions competent intermediaries, always useful for maintaining links between the various commands, became even more essential; yet in the headquarters of the different armies officers with the required sophistication and experience were not readily available. It was here that Rühle distinguished himself. As an emissary between the tsar, the Russian and Prussian commanders, and Bernadotte, who led a small but politically and militarily significant Swedish force, Rühle's quick intelligence and political agility enabled him to explain and when necessary defend the decisions and questions he conveyed back and forth. He was soon valued for his ability to interact with the men in charge as interpreter, advocate, even discreet arbiter. His part in assuring a degree of coordination between the Allies is noted in the major Wilhelmine biography of Blücher, which has remained the standard work of the field-marshal's life and career, in words that sum up Rühle's reputation as it was in 1813: "[he] was regarded as somewhat schoolmasterly and fantastical, but … [as an intermediary] in the spring campaign proved to be very useful."[69]

The immediate goals of the Allies were to establish themselves in eastern Germany, keep the build-up of French forces off balance, and bring Austria and the various German governments to their side. At the end of March, Russian and Prussian troops, supported in the north by Bernadotte's Swedes, crossed the Elbe on a broad front, while in Franconia Napoleon was assembling forces for an offensive to divide the new allies. Though outnumbered, Blücher attacked and gained territory. Eventually he was halted; but the French could not exploit their success beyond a limited advance, and the Battle of Gross Görschen ended as a moral and eventually strategic victory for the Allies. During the fighting Scharnhorst was hit in the leg; the wound became infected, and he died on 2 June, a loss that Prussia, her army now modernized under his leadership, bore more easily than could Clausewitz. Two days later Napoleon proposed a truce. It was signed for a period of seven weeks, and then extended further. Both sides wanted time to replace losses, reorganize their forces, and resolve political uncertainties. Negotiations lasted for more than two months, until it became clear that Napoleon would never settle for a reduced if still powerful France. Austria declared war on 11 August, and the addition of her armies gave the Allies a military superiority that proved decisive.

In the fall campaign, Clausewitz, now again with the Russo-German Legion, served in northern Germany, a secondary theater of war, the Legion, Swedish troops, and various other small forces under Bernadotte's overall command guarding the right flank of the Allied armies. For a time, Clausewitz acted as chief of staff of a force of some twenty-seven thousand men under Count Wallmoden-Gimborn, which covered Bernadotte's right flank against Davout, who from his base in Hamburg sought to divert as many Allied troops as possible from the main confrontation further south. Both Clausewitz and Pfuel contributed to the Legion's victory on the Göhrde, a forested area west of the Elbe, in which the Legion overran a badly outnumbered French force. Advancing further towards Hamburg and then turning north, the Legion defeated a Danish force in Holstein, a success for which Pfuel received the high Prussian decoration of *Pour le mérite*. In Blücher's headquarters meanwhile, Rühle once more proved his worth as a diplomatic emissary between the various commanders. In December 1813 he was promoted to lieutenant-colonel. A throat infection then kept him from further field service, and he did not take part in the final campaigns against Napoleon. Instead he was appointed commissioner general overseeing the rearmament of the various German states, another task that called for political suppleness. As an advisor to the Prussian delegates he attended the Congress of Vienna, and at the end of 1814 his name was mentioned as a possible tutor for the crown prince. Before Rühle was chosen, Clausewitz, who held this position earlier, was asked for his opinion on the appointment. He found both Rühle and another candidate suitable, but added that Rühle's "metaphysical views" frightened him.[70]

Between his administrative duties, Rühle continued to give free rein to his remarkable literary energies. One of his projects at the time was to revise the lectures he had planned to give in Dresden. They were published in 1814 as "A Fragment of a Series of Lectures on the Theory of the Art of War by R. v. L.," under the title *Vom Kriege* (*On War*), the title Clausewitz later chose for his own work.[71] In the lectures Rühle combined two of his favorite ideas, his conception of war as art, and what he regarded as the educational nature of war, its beneficial impact on society. A state's army, he believed, should be nationalized, and its people should be militarized. All men, whatever their class and occupation, should serve, so that a greater part of society could participate in executing and representing the martial force of the state. Rühle's *On War*, which opens with a discussion and rejection of Kant's conception and advocacy of eternal peace, was characterized shortly after his death in 1847 as "an apology of war ... no other work develops with equal clarity and an equally encompassing point of view such a clear understanding of the permanent necessity of war. [The work] thus ennobles the warrior's calling by raising it far above any moral misgivings."[72]

During the Spring campaign of 1814, as the Allies were forcing Napoleon back to Paris, Clausewitz served with the Legion in Belgium and Holland, and was its last commander. He reverted to Prussian service in April; Pfuel followed in December 1814, both with the rank of colonel. Clausewitz was still busy with the dissolution of the Legion in March 1815, when Napoleon returned from Elba. In the hurried mobilization of the Prussian field army under Blücher, with Gneisenau again as chief of staff, Pfuel was appointed one of his senior assistants, while Clausewitz became chief of staff of the 3rd Corps under General von Thielmann. On 2 May the preparations for what turned into the Waterloo campaign were interrupted by a mutiny of Saxon troops in the Allied army. As part of its political restructuring of western and central Europe after the reduction of the French Empire, the Congress of Vienna compelled Saxony, which abandoned Napoleon only at the last moment, to transfer two fifths of its territory and one half of its population to Prussia, which in turn gave up some of its recent Polish acquisitions to Russia. Late in April Frederick William ordered that the noncommissioned officers and privates of the Saxon corps of some fourteen thousand men, then stationed at Liège, be divided into a Prussian and a Saxon brigade, according to their place of birth in territory now Prussian or remaining Saxon, the Prussian brigade placed in the 2nd Corps under Lieutenant-General von Borstell. The Prussian newcomers were to delay taking the oath to their new sovereign until officially released from their previous allegiance. Instead hundreds of Saxons refused to follow orders. A few officers were assaulted, soldiers tried to enter Blücher's quarters, broke its windows, and wrecked Gneisenau's rooms. Blücher ordered the three battalions at the core of the mutiny disarmed, their flags burned, and the ringleaders shot. Unless the leaders were handed over he would have the battalions decimated.[73] Pfuel was sent to carry out the punishment. He succeeded in convincing several of the leaders to give themselves up, four of whom were executed, which avoided the decimation. Borstell, who refused to dishonor his troops by burning their flags, was relieved of his command, court-martialed after the campaign ended, and sentenced to six months' confinement in a fortress, after which he returned to service and his very successful career.

In the brief Waterloo Campaign Pfuel continued to serve on Gneisenau's staff. On 15 June he was sent to Wellington in Brussels, one of a number of emissaries and messengers going back and forth between the British and Prussian commanders, exchanges that nevertheless did not prevent a new breakdown in communication. The following day Blücher, believing Wellington nearer than he actually was, decided to defend his position at Ligny. Unable to withstand a series of determined assaults, he withdrew northeast towards Wavre, where Thielmann and Clausewitz prepared to meet a separate column of thirty-three thousand men under Grouchy, as Napoleon shifted to face Wellington. On 18 June Grouchy allowed himself to be involved in a day-long engagement that tied up and denied Napoleon forces he badly needed at Waterloo nine miles to the west, while Blücher reorganized his troops and began to push towards Wellington. A reconnaissance led by Pfuel showed that the eastern part of a heavily wooded area at the end of Napoleon's right wing was not strongly held, and soon after four in the afternoon of 18 June Prussian forces entered the wood and worked their way towards Plançenoit to the rear of the extended French position. After Wellington repulsed what Clausewitz termed the last, "desperate" attack of the Guards, and French units began to falter and withdraw, Pfuel drafted the Prussian communique announcing the victory.[74] By 29 June the Allies reached Paris. Pfuel was named commandant of the left bank, while Thielmann's corps with Clausewitz marched through the capital to the area of St. Germain and Fontainebleau, some units following remnants of the French army to the Loire until an armistice was concluded, and on 2 October the Second Peace of Paris was signed.

. . .

In the course of the army's demobilization, a new command on the Rhine was formed with Gneisenau as its head and Clausewitz his chief of staff. The command's responsibilities went beyond the strictly military to social and political issues brought about by fusing the old Prussian territories on the Rhine with new acquisitions gained at the Congress of Vienna and in the negotiations leading to the second Peace of Paris. Gneisenau and the senior members of his staff, most, like Clausewitz, having retained the political and military perspectives that had driven reform forward, were well suited to collaborate with the civil administration. It was at this time that Clausewitz linked his interest in the development of representative bodies and ministerial responsibility with a new expectation that Prussia, greatly strengthened by the outcome of the war, would replace the Habsburg Empire as the decisive power in Germany, a combination of liberal tendencies with belief in Prussia's German mission that came to be held by more than one of his contemporaries, Pfuel among them—not by Rühle, however, who never shared the more critical approach to monarchic absolutism of his intimate friends Kleist and Pfuel, let alone the activism that drove Scharnhorst and his close associates Tiedemann and Clausewitz. Rühle had not taken part in the efforts and conflicts of the Prussian military reforms, and his views in subsequent years were in line with those held by the conservative core of the army's leadership. In spite of his fantastic visions of war as an ethical and aesthetic enterprise, the king and his advisors recognized him to be immune to liberal tendencies, an appraisal that together with his energy and administrative ability assured him of an excellent career.

By contrast, the degree of flexibility and tolerance Gneisenau and his staff showed in the Rhineland, its population very different in its social, economic, and cultural character from the inhabitants of the Prussian core provinces, made them suspect to conservatives, who now that the war was over sought to reverse the innovations of the past decade. Gneisenau, unwilling to face new political conflicts, resigned his position in 1816. He was succeeded by a conservative, a political ally of Knesebeck, under whom Clausewitz did not want to serve. Gneisenau and other friends had already begun to consider Clausewitz for the open position of of the War Academy, which carried with it promotion to Major-General, and in 1818, after Frederick William thought it necessary to order an investigation into the candidate's moral and political character, Clausewitz was appointed.

His move to the War Academy brought Clausewitz into Rühle's orbit. During the Waterloo campaign, Rühle, who did not serve with the field army, had been promoted to Colonel and made a member, later the director, of the commission overseeing the curriculum of the War Academy. When peace returned he was attached to the War Ministry, became head of the section for military history, and following his promotion to Major-General in 1818 combined his expanded duties at the War Ministry and the General Staff with his position at the War Academy, which gave him an important voice in appointing faculty and shaping the teaching program, while Clausewitz as Director was responsible merely for the school's administration and discipline. Occasions for conflict inevitably arose; but however the two men felt about each other, their close association over many years seems never to have led to open disputes. At the same time, Clausewitz did not care for his administrative position, which kept him away from policy issues, an isolation only slightly ameliorated when in 1821 he was made an associate though not as Rühle a regular member of the Great General Staff. He was grateful for the isolation that allowed him to concentrate on writing; but his continued interest in a diplomatic appointment makes apparent how little he valued his position at the War Academy.

Pfuel, who like Rühle had not been in Prussian service during the years of reform and whose moderate political views were not generally known, was promoted to Major-General the same year as Clausewitz and Rühle, and became chief of staff of the 8th Corps.[75] During the following years he held a number of senior command and staff positions, one of his superiors characterizing him as faster when thinking than when riding, and it became apparent that he was being kept in mind for unusual assignments. A comparison of the respective positions Clausewitz, Pfuel, and Rühle had attained by the early 1820s reveals similarities—all held the same grade—but also differences, with Pfuel's reputation for versatility, Rühle firmly lodged in a position of power and influence in the army's central administrative sector, and Clausewitz holding an administrative post that might easily be a final appointment. How then to explain the article on Clausewitz that in 1822 appeared in a major German publication?

The encyclopedia that Friedrich Brockhaus began to publish in Leipzig in 1796, followed by a new edition every seven years or so, soon became, and remains today, a standard reference work in Germany. When the fifth edition appeared, the first volume, A–Cz, contained an article on Clausewitz's career that identifies him as "one of the most distinguished officers of the Prussian Army." His indebtedness and closeness to Scharnhorst and his work in reforming the army are noted, as are his contribution to "General Yorck's eternally memorable convention," his authorship of the *Outline of the Campaign of 1813* published by Brockhaus, "his distinguished service in the engagement at the Göhrde," as well as his current position as director of the War Academy. The article ends with the sentence, "Apart from the *Outline of the Campaign of 1813* mentioned above, Clausewitz has written several essays in military publications, in which the false theories of fashionable systems that try to base the conduct of war either on geometric figures or on geological analogies are astutely confronted."[76]

This account and its appearance in a major dictionary raise a number of questions. Why was Clausewitz singled out in a work that did not discuss other officers, apart from such already historical figures as Scharnhorst and Blücher—and, incidentally, Kleist since 1817—or, among the living, Gneisenau? Pfuel and Rühle are not mentioned in its pages. And to what publications does the concluding sentence refer? By 1822 Clausewitz had not yet published much. His 1805 review of Bülow's work was his only theoretical study in print so far; his articles on the campaign of 1806 and the *Outline of the Campaign of 1813* discuss strategic decisions only briefly and as part of the narrative. That Brockhaus had brought out Clausewitz's little book on 1813, which sold well, and made him known to the publisher, might have been the link that led to the article. But who was its author? The article's reference to Clausewitz's writings suggests a fellow officer, someone who had seen or might know of Clausewitz's service memoranda, was aware of his contribution to the *Reglement* of 1812, and heard his lectures on the Little War. Documentary evidence is lacking, but it might well have been Gneisenau, who continued to be Clausewitz's strongest supporter in the army.[77] Whatever the author's identity and sources, his concluding sentence is a remarkably early recognition of the importance of Clausewitz's ideas. Eleven years before the appearance of *On War* the article introduced him to the educated public as a military theorist who did not believe that war could be understood and conducted as an enterprise that responded predictably according to any practical doctrine or theoretical system. Whether Clausewitz benefited from his appearance in the pages of the Brockhaus encyclopedia is another question. The article is not mentioned in his surviving correspondence, and being praised in a work that more than once was subjected to cuts and changes by Prussian censors could only further antagonize Clausewitz's conservative critics.[78]

In 1830, the Prussian artillery, since the Reform era commanded by Prince August, was reorganized into three inspectorates, and in response to Clausewitz's continued wish for a new assignment he was relieved of the directorship of the War Academy and made head of the third inspectorate in Breslau. In July, a few weeks before he assumed his new position, revolution broke out in France, followed by revolution in Belgium; disturbances in Hesse, Saxony, and other German states; and at the end of November by an uprising against Russian rule in Poland. Civil strife might turn into war between states, and as a precautionary measure, Prussia mobilized 145,000 men under Gneisenau's command. At his request Clausewitz was appointed his chief of staff—an unexpected opportunity for him to move from the isolation of a military administrator to play a major role at the center of events. But the crises in western Europe were contained, and by the summer of 1831 Russian troops gradually subdued the Poles, which reduced the mission of Gneisenau's command to guard Prussia's eastern frontier, and after cholera broke out in Poland to implement measures to prevent the spread of the disease to Germany. In July the first cases were identified in Prussia. On 23 August, Gneisenau fell ill and died the following day. He was replaced by the arch-conservative Knesebeck, an appointment that Clausewitz experienced as "a thunderbolt from the clear sky."[79] At the beginning of October what remained of the Polish field army entered Prussian territory and surrendered, after which the Prussian covering force was demobilized, and Clausewitz returned to his inspectorate in Breslau. Shortly afterwards, on the morning of 16 November 1831, he fell ill with cholera, and died that evening.

Clausewitz's widow and her brother made his manuscripts available to the Berlin publisher Dümmler, who in 1832 began to bring out an edition of Clausewitz's writings in ten volumes, with *On War* in the first three. What seems to be the earliest review of *On War* was written by Rühle, and appeared in 1833 before the concluding parts of the work—Books VII and VIII—had been published, in the *Yearbooks for Philosophical* [or *Scientific*] *Criticism,* the organ of the Society for Philosophical Criticism [Sozietät für wissenschaftliche Kritik] that Hegel had founded in 1826.[80] Within a few years the society and its journal had become a force in German scholarly and intellectual life, the Prussian government began to give it some financial support, and it was allowed to hold its meetings in the reading room of the Royal Library in Berlin, even as it remained a nongovernmental institution. Its members included Goethe and Wilhelm von Humboldt, numerous officials and academics from the German states, and among senior officers both Pfuel, who reviewed a work on the war of 1812 in the *Yearbooks,* and Rühle.[81]

In 1829 Rühle's broad-ranging literary energies had led him to publish a pamphlet highly critical of Hegel's philosophy. Joining Rühle's work to another similarly hostile publication, Hegel started to write a response, but then, "in disgust at the shallowness of his critics," decided they did not deserve a reply—an episode that neither kept Rühle from contributing to the *Yearbooks* nor the editors from publishing his work.[82] Rühle's review of *On War* is representative of his writings in general—a vaguely structured mix of intelligence and phantasy, frequently abstract in sense and expression, and very long. Particular to the review is its author's rather cavalier treatment of Clausewitz's text. He never gives precise references, does not always cite accurately, and in a sort of intellectual enthusiasm that rises above narrow convention does not hesitate to combine widely separated passages into "sentences," which he then interprets. His review extends over three issues of the journal for a total of over six thousand words. It opens with two paragraphs that eulogize Clausewitz,

> departed in the heyday of his years, before he could give this work, which for many years had by preference occupied him, its completion and polish. Not only his closer friends, but all his comrades mourn him deeply ... [We] are indebted to him for having labored, as though sensing his early death, ... to bring enough of the results of his manifold experience and constant reflection to the light of day, so that his work will benefit the state and the educated world for years to come.

War, Rühle continues, is a difficult subject to study. Clausewitz, however, "combined two qualifications equally essential for the writer on war: *experience* gathered personally, and refined in contact with the most enlightened and tested experts, and secondly, a sufficient measure of *general education* to give him the firm conviction that a theory that meets the requirements of war is both feasible and needed."[83] He further asserts that Clausewitz's work is distinguished by the author's profound observation of reality, sound judgment, and "original, at times inspired ideas," yet he would not be surprised if *On War* were to enjoy less success than other books of this kind, a comment that leads Rühle to a discussion of the type of reader who tends to be interested in works on the theory of war. On the whole, he believes, this reader lacks the knowledge necessary for developing a sensible opinion about a matter "that is among the grandest and most difficult," a subject that cannot be studied by subjecting it to experiments, and that is made more confusing by the many poor theories to which it has been subjected. "Consequently it may be predicted that [*On*

War's] outstanding qualities—the author's unique point of view, his independent and frank judgment, his effort to achieve scientific accuracy, and the difference between his writings and other strategic doctrines ... —are just those that only a few readers will fully appreciate." Rühle adds, no doubt correctly, that the great majority of readers of military texts "are generally less interested in philosophical reasoning than in rules [*positive Didaktik*]."[84] He ends this first section of his review by quoting Clausewitz's Note of 10 July 1827 on his plans for revising *On War*, which Clausewitz concludes with the statement that despite the imperfections of his unrevised text he hopes an unprejudiced reader will find the manuscript contains ideas that may bring about a revolution in the theory of war. He himself, Rühle notes,

> educated in the same school as the author, with whom he was long associated in the service, and whom after years of close contact he may call a friend, not only fully shares the view stated at the end of the note, but goes so far in his partiality and belief in the theory basic to the author's work—the theory of their common teacher [i.e., Scharnhorst]—that he regards it as the only one so far that expresses the spirit of the new way of war and of the higher conduct of war developed by Frederick, by Napoleon and those who overcame him, a theory ... that will apply to the conduct of war in the future.[85]

In this long introduction, one third of the entire review, Rühle has scarcely touched on the specifics of the work he is discussing. He now lists the titles of the first six Books of *On War*, but adds that since Clausewitz regards only the opening chapter of Book I, which indicates the direction of the work as a whole, as complete, "it is the one to which we in our discussion must give preference."[86] He bases his summary of the chapter on Clausewitz's conception of war as the interaction of two living forces that mutually limit each other's effectiveness. "The original effective potential of each party, seen in isolation, is modified a) by the opponent's counteraction, b) by various events not dependent on the two opponents, most of which cannot be foreseen. Success therefore rests on predictive measurements of probability." The effectiveness of any action, Rühle continues, depends on its relation to the ultimate political goal, the spirit and attitude of the combatants, and the ability of the commander, "whose decisions must be the result of thinking through the various issues by weighing means, purpose, and probability of success against each other, and seeking to combine the particular acts and effects into a force directed at the common goal." This conceptualization, Rühle believes, "is enough to provide a sound basis for the totality of action [*reicht hin, um für das gesammte Thun und Wirken einen konsequenten Anhaltspunkt ... zu geben*]."[87] He adds, "anyone who wishes to take the trouble to make the comparison, will be convinced of the far-reaching analogy of this basic concept with the principles the reviewer proposed and attempted to develop in detail in his *Handbook for the Officer*," an assertion of breathtaking self-deception, which also seems to conflict with Rühle's earlier praise of Clausewitz's originality.[88]

Some mild criticisms of Clausewitz follow. Rühle supposes that in his intended revisions he would have made "a bit clearer" what he means by *absolute war*, would also have clarified "for the less gifted and less oriented reader" how various specifics are linked to the principal concepts or laws, would have given as well a fuller explanation of the principle of polarity, a principle the recognition of which, in all its forms, "this reviewer considers the first requirement of any theory and practice of war."[89] At present he does not understand why Clausewitz argues that because the two main forms of war, attack and defense, are of unequal strength, defense being the stronger, polarity cannot be applied to them—a point to which Rühle will return at the end of the review. He blends his analysis of the book with expansive musings on war and on the problems of studying it, streams of ideas and opinions in which the work under review nearly disappears. More than once he returns to his cherished concept of war as an art, and he repeatedly notes that readers of books on war tend to be ignorant about the subject—presumably he is thinking of civilians; but it would be surprising if many civilian readers of the *Yearbook* could have found their way through the intensely military thicket of Rühle's text. At the same time the flood of his language contains some intelligent and precise observations. He refers to the contradictory and changeable character of the elements of war, a constant fluidity that forms "a principal obstacle to those who attempt to teach the art of war scientifically and seek everywhere to give universally valid, positive rules."[90] To understand Clausewitz's work, he adds, it is not enough to memorize its contents. "One cannot simply adopt individual terms and isolated expressions." They all interact, affect, and change each other.[91] Or he observes that Clausewitz's "comprehension of the history of war and of the role of the commanding general ... derives mainly from his conviction that the conduct of war is closely linked to politics ... ."[92]

Rühle brings his discussion of *On War* to a close with two paragraphs, which in miniature combine the disparate elements that characterize the review as a whole: an intense but rather disorganized analysis of a few selected parts of the book, and an understanding of Clausewitz's method that nevertheless is throttled by the reviewer's tendency to combine a knowledge of reality with idealistic and ideological conclusions. The first of Rühle's two concluding paragraphs begins:

> The sixth book "Defense" is undoubtedly among the most successful sections of the work. With triumphant eloquence and cogent reasons [Clausewitz expounds] a fundamental principle, a statement of the greatest importance to mankind and to the political and moral justification of war: *"that of the two main forms of war*

> the defensive form is intrinsically stronger than the offensive," which is true both tactically and strategically. It applies both to a particular engagement, to the plan of operations and to the conduct of entire campaigns.

What Rühle takes as a "fundamental principle," he follows with a further quotation from Clausewitz, this one taken from chapter 26, *The People in Arms* of Book VI of *On War*, in which Clausewitz identifies the people in arms as a means of the defensive:

> A popular uprising should, in general, be considered an outgrowth of the way in which in our lifetime conventional barriers have been swept away by the elemental violence of war. It is, in fact, a broadening and intensification of the fermentation process known as war. Any state that uses it intelligently will, as a rule, gain some superiority over those who disdain its use.[93]

After citing this passage—a good example of the way Clausewitz's interpretation of historical reality contributes to his theoretical understanding—Rühle shifts to repeat and illustrate a very different point, one he had earlier made about Clausewitz's method: In the discussion of the use of battle in Book IV, he writes, Clausewitz makes the absolute statement "The major battle is … to be regarded as concentrated war, the center of gravity of the entire conflict or campaign.—There is then no factor in war that rivals the battle in importance, and the greatest strategic skill will be displayed in creating the right conditions for it, choosing the right place, time, and line of advance, and making the fullest use of its results."—a "sentence" that combines segments of *On War* several pages apart. Rühle continues by comparing Clausewitz's assertion of the supreme significance of the major battle with a contrary statement in Book VI, which, he finds, is equally correct—as he notes, the second absolute statement adds "balance and moderation" to the first absolute statement: "A government must never assume that its country's fate, its whole existence, hangs on the outcome of a single battle, no matter how decisive, for the strategic plans for defense can provide for [another means of fighting that is used in one of two ways:] a general insurrection, either as a last resort after a defeat or as a natural auxiliary before a decisive battle." We dare assert, Rühle continues, that

> the defensive form of war, waged by a state held together by wise laws, a just government, love of fatherland, and the innate superiority of the defensive over the advantages associated with the offensive—surprise, initiative, brilliant opening successes that impress public opinion and strengthen one's confidence—that all these elements acquire their keystone only when the people are armed, and their actions coordinated and harmonized with the machinery of the state and an extended system of defensive points. Not only in extreme cases, but under all conditions, in every circumstance of war, to arm the people is to gain an incalculable profit that cannot be equaled by other means.[94]

With these words the review abruptly ends. The phases of its concluding statement are worth retracing. It opens by declaring the strength of the defensive, proceeds to war waged by civilians, which takes operations out of complete control of the established authorities, from there to the interaction of two opposing absolutes, and ends by praising the superior *ethics* of the defense. By then, and with his characteristic mix of ethics and logic, Rühle has turned Clausewitz's analysis of the people's war as an effective military instrument into a paean of the higher morality. It is hardly necessary to say that this is not what Clausewitz had in mind. His recognition of the potential power of popular insurrection values ideology as a motivating force, but does not insist on its ethical grandeur. The motives of the fighters may be admirable, misguided, reprehensible, or a combination of all three. From his study of history and from events of his own time Clausewitz concluded that popular action, whether in the end effective or not, may be motivated by a variety of often contrary beliefs. It is not inevitably based on the existence of a "just government." Indeed popular action may oppose a government, whatever the nature of its policies. Rühle, by contrast, finds the ultimate strength of the people's war, as of defensive war as such, in its innate ethical superiority: To defend oneself is moral, to attack is not—which ignores the broad range of political motives and consequences that may lead to either attack or defense. Though he agrees with and admires Clausewitz's recognition that war is an extension of politics and policy, he neither takes note of the multiplicity of ways in which war and politics may relate, nor the implications of their relationship for strategy and operations. Possibly Rühle's personal experience, including years of resisting Republican and Imperial French expansion, had overcome his interest in objective, impersonal analysis, an approach in any case far from prominent in his work. He accepts some basic truths in the abstract; but whatever concepts he proclaims, when he traces their paths through the maze of real issues and conflicts he tends to succumb to ethical preconceptions—to what he believes should be, rather than to recognize and seek to understand what is. Certainly he was not alone in this. From Ranke on, the scholars of the Prussian Historical School, the first generation of which overlapped with the last decades of Rühle's life, "regarded history as an ethical process: the nations or states that prevailed were those embodying a higher morality."[95] But that is not how Clausewitz saw the past. In his discussion of *On War*, Rühle, on the contrary, allows his mix of objectivity and idealization to lead him far from Clausewitz's ideas, the ideas he is supposedly evaluating, a shamble of impressive formulations leading to contradictory conclusions, which makes one wonder what readers of the *Yearbooks* were able to take away from the review.

On War was not the only work Rühle discussed in the *Yearbooks of Philosophical Criticism*. For more than a decade he reviewed books for the journal: French and German titles on geography and on history and military history, as well as several works on the theory of war by Jomini, and one by Jomini's German disciple Willisen.[96] On the whole these discussions are more clearly organized, more of a piece, and give the reader a better grasp of the works' contents than does the review of *On War*, which in places appears to be written by an author of two minds. Evidently the more technical, less comprehensive, strictly military approach of the other works did not present Rühle with a similar challenge. His review of *On War*, in which his sense of realism is blurred and at times overwhelmed by sentiment, says more about the reviewer and perhaps also about the changing political conditions and cultural atmosphere in which he now lived, than it does about Clausewitz. It shows Rühle to be a representative of the mix of practical understanding and theories of war in which politics, strategy, and operations are mentioned without being fully integrated that largely characterized his and Clausewitz's generation of writers on war. His learned confusion enables us to gain a fuller picture of the professional and intellectual context out of which Clausewitz's work emerged. In some parts his discussion almost previews a common reception of Clausewitz's ideas by the following generations of scholars and soldiers, who too often abandoned Clausewitz's dialectical recognition of war, whether in policy or in the field, for the simpler pursuit of unitary concepts, which the writers of the late nineteenth century and beyond may have thought were better attuned than Clausewitz's classicistic reasoning to the age of industrialization, mass armies, and nationalism.

Despite his uncertain health, Rühle's energies as a writer and senior officer did not flag. In 1835 he was promoted to lieutenant-general. Two years later, after having headed the War Academy's curriculum committee for more than a decade, he also became the Academy's director, combining two positions that he and Clausewitz had held separately. In 1844 he was appointed inspector-general of military education and president of the army's officer's examination program. He died, still in service, in 1847. In his last years he as well as Pfuel, friends since fifty years earlier when they and Kleist came to know each other in the Potsdam garrison, provided reminiscences and documents to the author of the first full-scale biography of Kleist, the publication of which in 1848 was one sign among many signaling Kleist's entry into the pantheon of German literature.[97]

During the same decades Pfuel's career had gradually lifted him above the curve of the usual senior appointments. In 1830 he became commandant of Cologne, a position of some political complexity he continued to hold for the next eight years together with his other duties. The following year, four years before Rühle, he was promoted to lieutenant-general, and immediately afterwards, in January 1832, was sent to Neuchâtel, where political unrest had broken out. Neuchâtel or Neuenburg, a territory some twenty miles west of Berne on the northwest border of Lake Neuchâtel, was both a Swiss canton and since 1707 a hereditary possession of the Hohenzollern branch that reigned in Prussia, a remnant of the extreme territorial division of Germany, much of which had been eliminated in the political upheavals that began with the French Revolution and provisionally ended with the Congress of Vienna and Waterloo. At Neuchâtel, maneuvering between an aristocratic Prussian party and a democratic bourgeoisie, Pfuel managed to accommodate the institution of a more liberal regime, including a constitution and freedom of the press, without significantly limiting the sovereignty of the Prussian crown. With the concurrence of the Neuenburg council of state he was appointed governor, a position he retained for the next seventeen years, which required an annual visit to the principality without affecting his continued service in the Prussian Army, in which by 1848 he had become a senior general and holder of the highest decorations.

Early that year, after a period of political unrest, revolutions broke out across Europe. On 26 February a republic was proclaimed in France. Even earlier demonstrations and riots occurred in various German states, which soon spread to the Rhineland and from there to Berlin. On 2 March, Frederick William IV appointed Pfuel governor of Berlin, in these weeks the most challenging post in the army. Troops had been stationed throughout the city, and encounters between them and crowds holding meetings in the parks or demonstrating in the streets were now common and potentially incendiary. On 14 March Pfuel issued an order to the troops to act with restraint. The following day as an unruly crowd confronted a detachment of soldiers guarding the royal palace, Pfuel intervened at some personal risk and prevented the soldiers from firing into the crowd, an act for which he was reproved by the king's younger brother, the future William I.[98] On 18 March after the building of barricades led to street fighting in which 230 people were killed, the king agreed to some political demands of the insurgents—the drafting of a constitution, abolition of censorship—but also dismissed Pfuel. Six weeks later while conflicts continued unabated between conservatives, moderates, and radicals, supporters and enemies of a constitutional monarchy, between proponents of Prussia merging into Germany and adherents of an autonomous Prussia, Pfuel was sent to Poznan to prevent a threatened civil war between Germans and Polish nationalists in the formerly Polish territories. He did not soften Prussian policies, which the Polish opposition was too weak to oppose, but acted with sufficient political acumen to end, on 15 June, the state of siege that had been imposed.

The day before, the continuing crisis in Berlin led to an assault on the Berlin armory by workers and radical democrats, which was repelled by the bourgeois National Guard and military units, but the clear evidence of the breakdown of civil order brought down the government. The succeeding ministry lasted three months until it fell over the issue of the Prussian officer corps taking an oath to the constitution, a step the king rejected as an unacceptable interference in his prerogatives. On 21 September he appointed Pfuel minister-president and minister of war, which placed a general who had become known to favor moderate change at the center of government. Four days after his appointment Pfuel issued an order to the senior generals not to tolerate reactionary tendencies in the army, and to advance mutual understanding between the military and civilians—"the largest concession that a man of compromise could still wrest from the king."[99] As in his earlier political appointments Pfuel sought to find a path between opposing ideological and political factions; but he was unable to convince the king and his absolutist advisors of the value of a moderate constitution, and in October resigned with his cabinet. His ministry had always been regarded as temporary and transitional, one that might create links between at least some of the contending factions. But he proved unable to overcome the arch-conservative forces that now brought the revolution to an end by securing for the Crown the high measure of executive power it retained and employed up to the end of the First World War. Pfuel retired from the army in 1849. His past conflicts with the Crown did not preclude further honors. He was elected to the Prussian House of Representatives as a Liberal, but then entered the new House of Lords, and two years before his death in 1866 was awarded the rare highest class of the order *Pour le mérite,* the decoration he had originally received for the Russo-German Legion's campaign in Holstein in 1813. A year after his death a monument was erected in Berlin, honoring him—not for his military and political services, or his efforts to introduce a moderate degree of liberalism into the military monarchy, but for his early recognition of the value of athletics, particularly swimming, in modern life.

· · ·

Tracing Clausewitz's life and achievement against that of the other four learned officers with whom these pages compare him—Kleist and Tiedemann who died early, Rühle and Pfuel who outlived him for many years—makes possible a fuller examination of the conditions and circumstances in which he developed his ideas and wrote his works. Seeing Clausewitz against his four contemporaries deepens the contours of his life; his immediate social and cultural environment and the events he experienced help explain aspects of the general character and many specific passages of his historical and theoretical manuscripts. He and his four fellow officers shared much in common. Born into the Prussian service elite within a few years of each other, growing up and serving in the army, at times in the same or related sections, exposed to the same events, ideas, and tendencies at home and abroad, they early responded in thought and action to the cultural and political forces of their time, each reacting to his environment with his own point of view and his particular creative abilities. With all the differences that define individuals, each of the five may be taken as in various respects representative of his times, place, and occupation, each a man whose insights or errors his associates might be ready to share, from whom they could learn, or whose ideas they could reject.

Seen together the similar conditions and events that the learned officers faced in their first twenty years, and to a large extent throughout their lives, also magnifies their innate and eventual differences. At times they reacted to one another, as did Clausewitz when he met the challenge of Rühle's ideas in the chapter "Art of War or Science of War" in Book II of *On War;* or Rühle when he reviewed Clausewitz's *On War,* an evaluation in which he thoroughly misreads the work's arguments even as he emphasizes the commonality in concerns, ideas, and conclusions he detects between his own theories and those of Scharnhorst's fellow student and his deceased friend—as he characterized him. As the ideas and actions of the five became more clearly defined in maturity, the affinities that remained, no less than the further contrasts that emerged, sharpen our understanding of each man. All, to return only to this point, possessed a common-sense awareness of the links between war and politics, and all thought further about how one affects the other, although all but one tended to visualize a relatively simple progression of policy leading to military action and from there to political result, and gave insufficient thought to the many other interactions between these two major forces: how war in general might alter society, let alone the impact that specific policies and even particular events in the field—a striking victory, a shocking defeat, the burning of a town, the treatment of prisoners or the refusal to take them—could have on public opinion or the judgment of the men in power. But it was left to Clausewitz to convert the shared recognition of the tie between the use of violence and the goal violence is meant to achieve—a tie they could not fail to identify when as adolescents they experienced the wars of the French Revolution—into a concise definition that incorporated the whole range of war, its causes and its outcome, from the effect of a policy decision to go to war and the choice of a particular strategy, to the influence the action of soldiers in the field, far from the decision makers, might have on public opinion and affect government policy. His definition of war, verbally modest and intellectually matter-of-fact, as the continuation of politics by other means, Clausewitz was able to convert into a vastly effective tool with which to create a systematic theoretical understanding of how war and the reasons for it interact in policy, but also in other realms commonly thought of as purely military or purely civilian. Rühle, on the other hand, could not turn his strong awareness of causality, a relationship between policy and war he frequently discussed in his writings, into productive insights. He had acquired some of the pieces with which to construct a viable theory of armed conflict in the relation between states, but lacked others, or rather allowed broad, if not seriously considered views on a policy's ethical character to shape his analysis. To him, ethical policy meant defensive war, and so far as society at large was concerned, ethics were reduced in his mind to patriotism and the willingness to serve—a vision that more than once blinded him to conditions and events as they were, and led him in directions that left the reality he analyzed far behind.

The learned officers lived at a time of major change, members of an institution and engaged in activities that were more closely tied to this change, its ideas, and their social, political, and organizational consequences, than is often recognized. In important respects an armed force, with its place in the state, manpower policies, organization, tactical doctrine and strategic concepts, reflects not only the social, technological, and political or ideological realities of the times in which it exists, but also some of their dominant intellectual and cultural tendencies. This near relationship is sequentially illustrated by the history of the Prussian Army from its apotheosis at the end of the Seven Years' War to its disaster in 1806, which came close to causing the permanent dismantling of the state, only to be followed in the next years by the state's and the army's reform and resurgence. The Frederician military system, in its careful, realistic exploitation of the human and material resources available, organized and drilled to the far-reaching exclusion of any deviation from the basic design, was a model of eighteenth-century rationalism: a dependable, largely inert instrument in one man's hands—Kleist's "sword lifelessly hanging" from Frederick the Great's belt. The army's tactical system may be seen as an extreme example of its overall nature, a sensible response to the weapons technology of the day—though after the early 1790s, as land warfare took on a different form even while the military technology remained largely unchanged, the response driven to its ultimate mechanical precision became questionable—a body of procedures and formations often compared to a clockwork mechanism, a favorite simile for characterizing the Enlightenment's determination to impose sense, order, and efficiency onto the seeming confusion of reality—but at the price of pushing aside the disturbingly unique and irregular. That the smooth workings of the Prussian military clock were achieved not least by drill sergeants and officers using canes and sticks to beat the human components of the machine into mindless execution of the commands, however heavy the enemy's fire, was seen as a regrettable remnant of a past that writers of the Enlightenment termed barbaric, a time in which the individual was not yet disciplined by reason.

Not that the dominant tendencies of a period are ever universally shared. Society always includes voices separated from, even opposed to current insights or fashions. In unsurpassed depictions of the power of human emotion, the Enlightenment's great composers, painters, poets, and philosophers revealed and interpreted, fathomed and celebrated love, jealousy, ambition, hatred—realms often assuming forms that conflicted or only uneasily joined those of reason and of a new sense of humanity. But even these original minds were affected by worldviews encircled by faith in reason and progress, a sense of advancing that might combine with still firmly held religious beliefs, but an advance that was expected to pierce what was still impenetrable, and would eventually help human beings gain a truer, more reasonable sense of themselves and of the world in which they lived.

Some military theorists at the end of the century, expressing their faith in the scientific conduct of war, carried the rationalist ideal into the new age. Their search for laws to define, engage, and exploit the predictive nature of conflict was stimulated by its very opposite: the enormity of the changes that imperceptibly emerged until they burst into the open in the Wars of the French Revolution. Other writers responded not by denying or trying to eliminate what could easily seem as irrational, but by accepting its challenge. Change existed, it had to be understood, and it could be countered by selectively adapting some of its characteristics. Reactions like those of Scharnhorst, which enabled him to recognize and meet the new forces on their own terms, were too deeply grounded in his early years as an independent-minded outsider to have been caused by newly dominant cultural forces; but being in accord with historical and cultural change increased their resonance. The Prussian Army, after its old rationalistic nature had proved helpless before new forms of organized violence, not least in response to the urgings of Scharnhorst and the men who shared his conviction of what reality now demanded, paralleled this cultural shift by choosing reform—some of its members doing so with considerable hesitation. Not only the organization and tactical doctrine of the modernized army, but its conduct of war was molded to be in closer accord with new insights and attitudes emerging from the late Enlightenment and reaching maturity in the period of Classicism and early Romanticism. Examples are early steps of broadening responsibilities in the service and increasing its flexibility without weakening the organization's central authority—for instance the development of a General Staff that became more than a group of geographers and adjutants and led to a new, productive relationship between commanding officer and chief of staff; or a less mechanical tactical doctrine, made possible by and dependent on the beginnings of a different treatment of the rank and file.

More than a few members of the generation at the turn of the eighteenth to the nineteenth century became newly conscious of and intrigued by the power not only of the rational but also of its opposite, which showed itself too often to be denied or explained away, a power that could not be silenced in the name of reason, but demanded understanding. One of the learned officers, Rühle, could not find a clear path from the old to the new. Two of the others sought to express the widening insights of their age in complete formulations—one man in drama, the other in a body of theory that in the first instance identified the components of war and addressed their interaction, not sought the certain path towards victory. Both Clausewitz and Kleist argued against schematic thought and action, and both arrived at a deeper level of reality in their recognition of the permanent uncertainty of events, not least in episodes of conflict. That they pointed to the limits of the predictable did not mean they denied the value of schooled forms of action and reaction—they were far too cognizant of the impediments in the path of any effective challenge and response—but they asserted their belief in the emotional and intellectual ability of human beings to deal with infinite change and variety, and, further, insisted that any doctrine should give the individual appropriate space in his area of action. Clausewitz and Kleist achieved this understanding without influencing each other. Even if Clausewitz did read *The Prince of Homburg* or others of Kleist's works, which cannot be said with certainty though he undoubtedly knew of them, the core of his ideas was already in place. The works of one man were not the "source" of the other. Rather, each in his own way and for his particular purposes made use of ideas and attitudes that rose to full strength in German and European culture towards the end of the eighteenth century, and each man applied them to matters of his greatest concern. And for both, the reality of conflict—whether within the individual, between them, between the individual and his environment, or between social and political entities—was not only an inevitable part of existence, but also a key to its understanding. For later generations to note the common cultural and intellectual starting points from which Kleist and Clausewitz approached these issues may lead to a clearer recognition of how their work developed and possibly also to its character.

What Kleist and Clausewitz wrote are impressive examples of the power ideas may gain when they are attached to broad issues: two works, one aesthetic, the other theoretical—both among the great nineteenth-century interpretations of armed conflict, its place in society and in the life of the individual—originated in the same years in the minds of two men, whose similar cultural, social, and professional antecedents helped them find the concepts and perspectives their time had to offer for their purposes, and apply these notions and insights to matters of their deepest concern. In *The Prince of Homburg* Kleist reveals how a few men and women react to war, and by way of war to life, its dangers and its promise. Homburg, the elector, Natalie, the officers and soldiers of Brandenburg are particular individuals faced with and accepting specific challenges. But their uniqueness stands for the uniqueness of others. In *On War* Clausewitz attempts an analysis of the motives, measures, and dynamic that in many different forms are present in armed conflict between opposing forces, which themselves assume a multitude of structures—a tribe, a state, divisions in a state and society that lead to uprisings and civil war— forces that in their composition and function are impersonal, but at every level are affected by and affect the individual, and to the analytic observer reflect major truths of human nature.

Creativity and originality always include the recognition, positive or critical, of relevant elements, capacities, and powers in the individual's time and culture. The old helps shape the new, whether in a dialectical or more organically consequential process. The historical and cultural context in which Kleist and Clausewitz lived, helped propel and mark everything they wrote, as their creative intelligence found what they needed, rejected what they opposed, and pushed their thought into the unexplored. They did not say the last word to be said about the matters they addressed—a concept of the absolute and definitive that Clausewitz would have rejected as absurd. But they gave rise to ideas that in form and substance were not only new as they reached from the realities of war to their aesthetic and theoretical understanding. The emotional and intellectual energy with which each man charged his work, created his ideas, and shaped their formulations, also integrated them into coherent systems—a drama, a theory—that carried their work beyond the limit of the times out of which they came.

Notes

1. After the Institute expanded, Scharnhorst outlined its organization and courses in *Verfassung und Lehreinrichtung der Akademie für junge Offiziere, und des Instituts für die berlinische Inspection,* Berlin, 1805. See also Georg Heinrich Klippel, *Das Leben des Generals von Scharnhorst,* I–III, Leipzig, 1869–1871; Max Lehmann, *Scharnhorst,* Leipzig, 1886; and Charles Edward White, whose *The Enlightened Soldier: Scharnhorst and the* Militärische Gesellschaft *in Berlin, 1801–1805,* New York, 1989, a good study of Scharnhorst and the Military Society, also contains an informative chapter and extensive references on the Institute and its curriculum.
2. Gerhard Scharnhorst, *Handbuch für Offiziere in den anwendbaren Theilen der Krieges-Wissenschaften,* Hannover, 1787–90; Gerhard Scharnhorst, *Militärisches Taschenbuch zum Gebrauch im Felde,* Hannover, 1792.
3. "Entwicklung der allgemeinen Ursachen des Glücks der Franzosen in dem Revolutions- kriege." Beatrice Heuser, *Reading Clausewitz,* London, 2002, 9, errs in stating that the essay was written together with Friedrich von der Decker [sic]. Decken, a Hanoverian officer who reached senior rank, was an intelligent defender of the military organization of late absolutism, and far too conservative to be the essay's coauthor. Despite his political views he and Scharnhorst were lifelong friends. The two coedited the *Neue Militairische Journal* in which the group of articles appeared, in an introductory note of which Scharnhorst names himself as the essay's sole author. See the reprinted text and the editorial introduction (192–94) in Gerhard von Scharnhorst, *Militärische Schriften,* ed. Colmar v. d. Goltz, Dresden, 1891. On Decken, see my *Yorck and the Era of Prussian Reform,* Princeton, 1966, 90–94, particularly note 127.
4. In his brilliant fragment, *Scharnhorst: Schicksal und geistige Welt,* Wiesbaden, 1952, 58, Rudolf Stadelmann points out that the two principal agents in the negotiations that brought Scharnhorst to Prussia were themselves newcomers, one transferred from Württemberg, the other from Brunswick.

5. Klippel, *Das Leben*, III, 550.
6. Carl von Clausewitz, "Über das Leben und den Charakter von Scharnhorst," *Historisch-politische Zeitschrift*, I (1832) 70–71. The article was published by Ranke in the year after Clausewitz's death.
7. "Auflösung der 26ten Aufgabe," in Carl von Clausewitz, *Schriften–Aufsätze–Studien–Briefe*, ed. Werner Hahlweg, Göttingen, 1966–1990, I, 57–58. My earlier brief discussion of this document in *Clausewitz and the State*, 78, did not recognize the broader implications of Clausewitz's answer.
8. See the fifth essay below.
9. A document that surfaced while the present work was in the press further confirms Clausewitz's early interest in studying human behavior and examining the problems of understanding others and oneself. It is an essay, unknown until now, of some 540 words, dated "August 1802," which he wrote as a student at the Institute of the Military Sciences in Berlin. The essay does not address military matters and is untitled. Its contents are indicated by the two opening sentences: "A great danger that often confronts decent individuals is to make harsh judgments of small faults and weaknesses in others—presumably out of their eagerness for the good. One usually finds that the very flaws that least appeal to such people are the ones they least forgive in others." I am indebted to Bernd Domsgen and Olaf Thiel of the *Freundeskreis Clausewitz* in Burg, for sending me images of the document.
10. Scharnhorst, *Militärische Schriften*, 194.
11. Ibid.
12. Max Lehmann, *Scharnhorst*, I, 319, 525.
13. 13 Peter Paret, "*Kleist* and Clausewitz: A Comparative Sketch," in *Festschrift für Eberhard Kessel zum 75. Geburtstag*, ed. Heinz Duchardt and Manfred Schlenke, Munich, 1982.
14. A detailed biography of Tiedemann does not exist, but he is frequently mentioned in documents of the time and in the scholarly literature. See also Joachim Niemeyer's article, "Carl Ludwig von Tiedemann," in the *Altpreussische Biographie*, Marburg, 1984, IV, 1164.
15. Hans Joachim Kreutzer, *Heinrich von Kleist*, Munich, 2011, 18.
16. On Pfuel, see the articles in the *Allgemeine Deutsche Biographie* and in Kurt von Priesdorff, *Soldatisches Führertum*, IV, Hamburg, 1937. Bernhard von Gersdorff has written a brief narrative biography, *Ernst von Pfuel*, Berlin, 1981. Pfuel also figures in biographies of Kleist, and in historical works on Prussia in the Revolution of 1848.
17. On Rühle, see especially his writings, and the anonymous, well-informed 65-page biography with 25 additional pages of documentation, *General-Lieutenant Rühle von Lilienstern*, in the Beiheft of the *Militair-Wochenblatt*, October–December, 1847, written in highly literary German by a knowledgeable, evidently senior officer, identified in an endnote, 194, as someone who was not the general's personal friend, but knew and served with him. Remarkably for a biography of a senior officer in an official army periodical (of which Rühle was one of the two founders), the text is a serious account of his career, containing both favorable and critical judgments. For additional information on Rühle, see the entries on him in the *Allgemeine Deutsche Biographie* and in Priesdorff's *Soldatisches Führertum*, IV, as well as biographies of Heinrich von Kleist.
18. Scharnhorst to Friedrich von der Decken, April 21, 1807, *Scharnhorst-Briefe an Friedrich von der Decken, 1803–1813*, ed. J. Niemeyer, Bonn, 1987, 127. For the earlier quotation, see Reinhard Höhn, *Revolution–Heer–Kriegsbild*, Darmstadt, 1944, 49. See also, ibid., 386–89, 462–64, 467.
19. See below, xyz.

20. Untitled brief essay, dated 1803, in Carl von Clausewitz, *Politische Schriften und Briefe*, ed. Hans Rothfels, Munich, 1922, 2. The same essay, with minor changes, and under the title "Nationalstolz," is included in Carl von Clausewitz, *Geist und Tat*, ed. Walther M. Schering, Stuttgart, 1941, 11.
21. Letter of 19 March 1799, to his former tutor Christian Ernst Martini, cited in Kreutzer, *Heinrich von Kleist*, 14.
22. Anonymous, "*General-Lieutenant Rühle von Lilienstern*," 126.
23. Rühle's answer to the Assignment is reprinted in ibid., 127.
24. Ibid. The elevated German text defeats any attempt at an exact translation: "[D]ie Befestigung der für das ganze Dasein entscheidende Geistesrichtung ... welche eine vorzugsweise Befriedigung des Lebens in der Auffassung seiner Erscheinungen mit dem Lichte der Ideen findet."
25. On Clausewitz's adoptions from Kant by way of Kiesewetter, see also my *Clausewitz and the State*, 154 nn161–62.
26. Heinrich von Kleist to Rühle, End of November or December 1805, *Kleists Sämtliche Werke*, V Arthur Eloesser, *Heinrich von Kleists Leben, Werke und Briefe*, Leipzig, n.d., 248.
27. Eberhard Kessel published these notes under the title, Carl von Clausewitz, *Strategie aus dem Jahr 1804, mit Zusätzen von 1808 und 1809*, Hamburg, 1937. See also my *Clausewitz and the State*, 89–94.
28. Heinrich von Bülow, *Lehrsätze des neuern Krieges*, Berlin, 1805; Carl von Clausewitz, "Bemerkungen über die reine und angewandte Strategie des Herrn von Bülow," *Neue Bellona* 9, no. 3 (1805).
29. 29 Ibid., 273–74. The noun Clausewitz uses, "Ausbildung," often translated as instruction or education, may here be more correctly translated as "development," or more specifically as "improvement" or even "maturation."
30. R. v. L., *Bericht eines Augenzeugen von dem Feldzuge der während den Monaten September und Oktober 1806 ... Königl. Preussischen ... Truppen*, Tübingen, 1807. Scharnhorst to Clausewitz, 27 November 1807, in *Scharnhorsts Briefe*, ed. Karl Linnebach, I, Munich, 1914, 335.
31. Clausewitz, "Historische Briefe über die grossen Kriegsereignisse im Oktober 1806," *Minerva* 1 (January and February 1807) and 2 (April 1807).
32. Carl von Clausewitz, *Principles of War*, trans. and ed. Hans Gatzke, Harrisburg, 1942. The tutorials are discussed in my *Clausewitz and the State*, 193–99.
33. On the committee preparing the *Reglement* of 1812 and Clausewitz's part in its work, see my *Yorck and the Era of Prussian Reform*, 179–90.
34. R. v. L., *Hieroglyphen oder Blicke aus dem Gebiete der Wissenschaft in die Geschichte des Tages*, Dresden, 1808. A second, expanded edition appeared in 1811.
35. *Pallas: Zeitschrift für Staats- und Kriegskunst* 1 and 2, 1808–10.
36. Heinrich von Kleist, "Prolog," *Phöbus*, ed. Helmut Sembdner, Darmstadt, 1961, 3. Translations of Kleist's texts are my own.
37. On this episode, see also Katharina Mommsen, *Kleists Kampf mit Goethe*, Heidelberg, 1974, 35–41.
38. Hans Joachim Kreutzer, "... und Frieden ist die Bedingung doch von allem Glück," in *Jahrbuch der Bayerischen Akademie der Schönen Künste*, X, Munich, 1996, 128. See also my essay, "Kleist und Clausewitz," 135.
39. Heinrich von Kleist, Michael Kohlhaas, *Sämtliche Werke*, ed. Arthur Eloesser, IV, Leipzig, n.d., p. 3.
40. Recollection of the historian Friedrich Christian Dahlmann, in *Heinrich von Kleists Lebensspuren*, ed. Helmut Sembdner, Bremen, 1957, 233. Clausewitz called Knesebeck

"Scharnhorst's and my own sworn enemy." See also my essay, "Fontane und der nicht gegenwärtige Clausewitz," in *Fontane Blätter* 69 (2000).
41. With the poem Kleist once again suffered disappointment. The French victory at Wagram prevented its publication. It was not printed until two years after his death, when at the beginning of the Wars of Liberation, Pfuel published it in Berlin. See Georg Minde-Pouet in Kleist, *Germania an ihre Kinder*, Berlin, 1918, 12.
42. J. J. Rühle von Lilienstern, *Reise mit der Armee im Jahre 1809*, I–III, Rudolstadt, 1810–1811.
43. Carl von Clausewitz, *On War*, I, ch. 3, "Art of War or Science of War," 148–50. Clausewitz writes, "war does not belong to the realm of arts and sciences; rather it is part of man's social existence." He concludes, war like any other subject "that does not surpass man's intellectual capacity, can be elucidated by an enquiring mind, and its internal structure can to some degree be revealed. That alone is enough to turn the concept of theory into reality," 149–50.
44. Rühle, *Reise mit der Armee*, III, 47–50.
45. Anonymous, "General-Lieutenant Rühle von Lilienstern," *Militair-Wochenblatt*, Beiheft, October-December, 1847, p. 142.
46. Cabinet Order of 11 September 1811, in Sembdner, *Heinrich von Kleists Lebensspuren*, 341.
47. Ibid., 484, 486, 490, etc.
48. The best edition and a remarkable reconstruction of Kleist's development of the manuscript and its subsequent history is *Heinrich von Kleist, Prinz Friedrich von Homburg*, ed. Richard Samuel with the assistance of Dorothea Coverlid, Berlin, 1964. The following quotations from the play are in my translation. A complete translation of the text is included in David Constantine ed. and trans., *Selected Writings: Heinrich von Kleist*, London, 1997.
49. Frederick the Great, "Mémoires pour servir à l'histoire de la Maison de Brandebourg," *Œuvres de Frédéric le Grand*, Berlin, 1846, 75–76.
50. The significance of the psychological motif has long been recognized in Kleist scholarship. For an example in the English-language literature, see Hilda Meldrum Brown, *Heinrich von Kleist*, Oxford, 1998, 364, etc. A recent thorough and consequential treatment of this central aspect of the play is Walter Hinderer's fine essay "Zweideutige Machtspiele im Hause Brandenburg," in the Program Booklet of the Salzburger Festspiele, 2012, *Heinrich von Kleist, Prinz Friedrich von Homburg*, Salzburg, 2012.
51. Act III, Scene 1.
52. Act III, Scene 5.
53. Act IV, Scene 1.
54. Act V, Scene 5.
55. Act V, Scene 10.
56. Act V, Scene 11.
57. Hinderer, 70.
58. On Rüchel's fatal delay at Jena see my book, *The Cognitive Challenge of War*, Princeton, 2009, Map 3 on 20, 23–24.
59. Friedrich Gundolf, *Heinrich von Kleist*, Berlin, 1922, 141.
60. Letter of April 28, 1812, *Scharnhorsts Briefe*, ed. Karl Linnebach, Munich-Leipzig, 1914, I, 428.
61. Clausewitz, *Schriften–Aufsätze–Studien–Briefe*, I, 678–750.
62. Clausewitz, *Politische Schriften und Briefe*, 1. The editor dates this study from 1803.
63. Gabriele Venzky, *Die Russisch-Deutsche Legion in den Jahren 1811–1815*, Wiesbaden, 1966, 74–5.

64. Anonymous, *Rückzug der Franzosen,* St. Petersburg [Berlin], 1813.
65. On the Convention of Tauroggen, see my *Yorck and the Era of Prussian Reform,* 191–96, and my *Clausewitz and the State,* 229–31.
66. Carl von Clausewitz, *Übersicht des Feldzugs vom Jahre* 1813, Leipzig, 1813.
67. For the book Rühle also chose the title of Scharnhorst's longer work *Handbuch für den Offizier.*
68. Anonymous, "General-Lieutenant Rühle von Lilienstern," 134.
69. Wilhelm von Unger, *Blücher,* Berlin, 1908, II, 61.
70. Letter of 21 December 1814 to Gneisenau, Carl von Clausewitz, *Schriften,* II 1, p 161.
71. Rühle von Lilienstern, *Vom Kriege: Ein Fragment aus einer Reihe von Vorlesungen über die Theorie der Kriegskunst,* Frankfurt a. M., 1814. The title *Vom Kriege* was not uncommon in the military literature of the time, e.g., in the 1790s the future Lieutenant-General Georg Wilhelm von Valentini wrote *Vom kleinen Kriege,* a manual on the „little war," which under somewhat different titles achieved six editions, and later a large work, *Lehre vom Kriege,* 1820–22, a technical, unsystematic compendium. On Valentini, whom Clausewitz called "the schoolmaster," see my *Clausewitz and the State,* 192–93.
72. Anonymous, "General-Lieutenant Rühle von Lilienstern" 142, 159.
73. Gersdorff, *Ernst von Pfuel,* 74.
74. Carl von Clausewitz, 1815.
75. Priesdorff, *Soldatisches Führertum,* IV, 398.
76. I am indebted to Bernd Domsgen and Olaf Thiel of the Freundeskreis Clausewitz in Burg, for calling my attention to this article.
77. As suggested by John Shy.
78. A briefer article, with the same concluding sentence, appeared in the 1827 edition of the encyclopedia.
79. See my *Clausewitz and the State,* 42.
80. Rühle von Lilienstern, "Vom Kriege. Hinterlassenes Werk des Generals Carl v. Clausewitz," *Jahrbücher für wissenschaftliche Kritik,* II, nos. 26–28, August 1833, columns 201–206, 209–215, 217–223. I briefly comment on the review in *Clausewitz and the State,* 312.
81. On the history and content of the *Yearbooks,* see the collection of essays introduced by Christoph Jamme, *Die Jahrbücher für wissenschaftliche Kritik,* Stuttgart–Bad Cannstadt, 1994. Rühle and Pfuel are briefly mentioned in the volume, but Rühle's review of *On War* is not discussed.
82. Hegel to Daub, 27 September 1829, *Briefe von und an Hegel,* ed. Johannes Hoffmeister, Hamburg, 1954, III, 273, 446.
83. Rühle von Lilienstern, "Vom Kriege. Hinterlassenes Werk," 26, columns 201–202.
84. Ibid., columns 203–204.
85. Ibid., columns 205–206.
86. Ibid., column 209.
87. Ibid., no. 27, column 210.
88. Ibid., column 211.
89. Ibid., column 212.
90. Ibid., column 214.
91. Ibid., column 214.
92. Ibid., no. 28, column 218.
93. Ibid., column 222. In the last sentence of the quoted text, Rühle changes Clausewitz's *Volk* ("People") to "State."
94. Ibid., columns 222–223.

95. Felix Gilbert, "Introduction," in Otto Hinze, *The Historical Essays of Otto Hintze*, ed. Felix Gilbert, New York, 1975, 5.
96. E.g., Rühle's extensive review article in the *Jahrbücher für wissenschaftliche Kritik*, I, nos. 45–47, March 1831.
97 Eduard von Bülow, *Heinrich von Kleists Leben und Briefe*, Berlin, 1848. The major contributions by Rühle and Pfuel are acknowledged in the author's introduction, vi.
98 The incident is reconstructed in Konrad Feilchenfeld, *Varnhagen von Ense als Historiker*, Amsterdam, 1970, 256–57.
99. Thomas Nipperdey, *Deutsche Geschichte, 1800–1866*, Munich, 1984, 649.

Illustrations

Gerhard Johann von Scharnhorst. Statue by Christian Daniel Rauch, Berlin, 1819–1822, today in front of the Staatsoper. Photograph by Suzanne Aimée Paret.

Carl von Clausewitz. Lithograph by Franz Michelis the younger after a painting by Wilhelm Wach, 1830. From the collection of Peter Paret.

Carl Ludwig von Tiedemann. Black and white miniature by an unidentified artist. From Carl von Clausewitz, *Schriften-Aufsätze-Studien-Briefe,* ed. Werner Hahlweg, I, Vandenhoeck und Ruprecht, Göttingen 1966, vol. 45 of *Deutsche Geschichtsquellen des 19. und 20. Jahrhunderts,* ed. Die Historische Kommission bei der Bayerischen Akademie der Wissenschaften.

Johann Jacob Rühle von Lilienstern. Lithograph by an unidentified artist. From K. von Priesdorff, *Soldatisches Führertum,* vol. IV, Hansa Verlag, Hamburg, 1937.

Adolph Heinrich Ernst von Pfuel. Painting by an unidentified artist. From K. von Priesdorff, *Soldatisches Führertum*, vol. IV, Hansa Verlag, Hamburg, 1937.

Heinrich von Kleist. Engraved by H. Sagert after a miniature by Peter Friedel, 1801, as frontispiece of Eduard von Bülow, *Heinrich von Kleist's Leben und Briefe*, Verlag von Wilhelm Besser, Berlin, 1848. From the collection of Peter Paret.

Clausewitz (Carl von), kön. preuß. Generalmajor, Director der allgemeinen Kriegsschule in Berlin, einer der ausgezeichnetsten Officiere der k. preuß. Armee, ist am 1sten Juni 1780 in Burg geboren, wo sein Vater als pensionirter Officier lebte. Schon im J. 1792 trat er als Junker in Dienst, machte als solcher die Feldzüge vom J. 1793 u. 1794 mit, benutzte die darauf folgenden Jahre, um sich durch Selbstbildung zur berliner Kriegsschule vorzubereiten, die er dann in den J. 1801 bis 1803 besuchte. Hier lehrte Scharnhorst, der dieser Anstalt einen neuen Geist einzuhauchen verstand und ihm verdankt Clausewitz, den er besonders auszeichnete und sich auf das freundschaftlichste mit ihm verband, die Grundlage seiner militärischen Bildung. In dem unglücklichen Feldzug vom J. 1806 begleitete Clausewitz den Prinzen August als Adjutant, und wurde in Folge der Affaire von Prenzlow als Gefangener mit nach Frankreich abgeführt. Dann diente Clausewitz bis zum J. 1812 als Major im Generalstabe, und war speciell dem Gen. v. Scharnhorst in dessen Bureau, das mit den später so bekannt gewordenen heilsamen Einrichtungen und Vorbereitungen zu dem nachmaligen Befreiungskriege beschäftigt war, attachirt. Außerdem gab er dem Kronprinzen von Preußen und dem Prinzen Friedrich der Niederlande Unterricht in den Kriegswissenschaften. Beim Ausbruch des russ. Kriegs nahm Clausewitz seinen Abschied, trat in russ. Dienste und machte den Feldzug als Oberquartiermeister bis Kaluga mit und wurde von hier zur Wittgensteinschen Armee versetzt, die sich an der Düna behauptet hatte. Als diese Armee im December dem Macdonaldschen Corps in den Rücken fiel, was die ewig denkwürdige Convention des Generals York herbeiführte, wurde Clausewitz auf den Wunsch Yorks dabei zum Unterhändler gebraucht. Die Campagne vom J. 1813 machte Clausewitz noch als russ. Generalstabs-Officier im Blücherschen Hauptquartier mit, und

Clauzel de Coussergues Clemens 665

schrieb während des Waffenstillstandes auf Gneisenaus Veranlassung die „Übersicht des Feldzugs vom J. 1813" (Glatz, und im Druck wiederholt Leipzig b. Brockhaus 1814), welche mit großem Beifall aufgenommen und lange Gneisenau zugeschrieben wurde. Nach Bildung der sogenannten russ. deutschen Legion, die zum Wallmodenschen Corps in Mecklenburg stieß, wurde Clausewitz zum Chef des Generalstabs dieses Corps ernannt und fand Gelegenheit, sich bei dem Treffen an der Görde vortheilhaft auszuzeichnen. Im J. 1815 trat Clausewitz in den preuß. Dienst zurück, und als Chef des Generalstabes des 3ten Corps unter Thielmann angestellt, das sich bekanntlich am Tage von Waterloo bei Wavre gegen Grouchy schlug. Nach dem Frieden war Clausewitz erst beim General-Commando am Rhein, und wurde dann zum Director der allgemeinen Kriegsschule ernannt. Außer jener Übersicht des Feldzugs vom J. 1813 rühren mehrere Aufsätze in militärischen Zeitschriften von Clausewitz her, in denen die falschen Theorien der Modesysteme, welche die Kriegführung im Großen bald auf geometrische Figuren, bald auf geologische Analogien gründen wollten, mit vielem Scharfsinn bekämpft werden.

"Clausewitz" in the *Allgemeine deutsche Real-Encyclopädie*, vol. 1, section 1, 1822.

Jahrbücher für wissenschaftliche Kritik.

August 1833.

XXXVIII.

Vom Kriege. Hinterlassenes Werk des Generals Carl v. Clausewitz. Erster Theil 1832. Zweiter Theil 1833. Berlin, bei Ferd. Dümmler. Oktav. Auch unter dem Titel: Hinterlassene Werke des Gen. Carl v. Clausewitz über Krieg und Kriegführung. Erster und zweiter Band u. s. w.

Als eines der schmerzlichsten Opfer, welche die vom Orient her ganz Mitteleuropa verheerend heimsuchende Seuche dem Preußischen Staate abgedrungen, wurde der Verf., (seinem auf gleiche Art kurz vorangegangenen Freunde, dem Feldmarschall Grafen Gneisenau, allzuschnell nachfolgend,) in der Blüthe seiner Jahre abberufen, ehe er diesem Werke, das ihn seit längerer Zeit vorzugsweis beschäftigt hatte, die letzte Ausbildung und äußere Vollendung zu geben vermochte. Nicht nur von nähern Freunden, sondern, als eine Zierde des Heeres von der Gesammtheit seiner Standesgenossen mit gleich reger Theilnahme betrauert, muß man es ihm Dank wissen, daß er, gleichsam im Vorgefühl seines frühen Scheidens, darauf bedacht gewesen ist, wenigstens die Ergebnisse vielseitiger Erfahrung und unausgesetzten Nachdenkens, in den letzten Jahren seines Lebens so weit zu Tage zu fördern, daß sein geistiges Wirken noch für späte Zeiten dem Staate und der gebildeten Welt lebendig forterhalten wird.

Es giebt hochbegabte und vom Schicksal ungewöhnlich begünstigte Naturen, welche das Erstaunenswürdige vollbringen, ohne sich der Beweggründe ihres Handelns selbst klar genug bewußt geworden zu sein, — am wenigsten auf solche Weise, daß sie vermöchten, es in Form allgemein ansprechender Lehre in Worte zu kleiden. Insonderheit gehört es zur Eigenthümlichkeit des Krieges, daß die, welche sich seinem Dienste

geweiht, selten Muße, Neigung oder äußeres Geschick besitzen, dieses für die menschliche Gesellschaft so bedeutsame Phänomen, (welches sich doch wiederum fast allen Anderen, die sich nicht unmittelbar in seinen Strudel stürzen, ganz unzugänglich und verborgen erhält) seinem ursächlichen Zusammenhange und innerem Wesen nach dermaßen zu ergründen und offenbar zu machen, daß es dem menschlichen Geiste, als Gegenstand der Erkenntniß und eines zweckgemäßen Handelns, gehörig und in gleichem Maaße wie andere Verhältnisse des Lebens unterworfen würde. In dem Verfasser fanden sich zwei zum militärischen Schriftsteller gleich nothwendige Hauptelemente auf glückliche Weise vereinigt: einmal, eigne *Erfahrung* im persönlichen Geschäftsbereiche eingesammelt, und im Umgange mit den erleuchtetsten und bewährtesten Sachverständigen geläutert; und zweitens, ein solcher Grad *allgemeiner wissenschaftlicher Bildung*, um nächst dem genugsamen Erkennen des der Praxis eigenthümlichen Bedürfens, die Ueberzeugung von der Möglichkeit und Unentbehrlichkeit einer diesem Bedürfen entsprechenden Theorie in sich fest begründet zu haben.

Das Werk liefert unzweideutige Beweise einer scharfsichtigen und tiefeindringenden Beobachtungsgabe, und eines nicht bloß natürlich gesunden, sondern auch zu nahmhafter Reife gediehenen Urtheils. Solchen Urtheils nämlich, das von dem Ballast, der durch verjährte Vorurtheile festgewurzelten (oder wie eine Art Modethorheit selbst die Mehrzahl der ausgezeichnetsten Feldherrn und Kriegsgelehrten influenzirenden,) theoretischen und praktischen Pedantismen frei geworden, und alle illusorischen Verbrämungen des wirklichen Sachverhältnisses verschmähend, nur nach Wahrheit und innerlich konsequenter Begründung strebt. Das Werk zeichnet sich aus durch originelle und zum Theil geniale Ansichten, durch einen erhabenen Standpunkt, und durch einen Schatz praktischer, nicht nur aus dem engeren Kreis des speziell

Jahrb. f. wissensch. Kritik. J. 1833. II. Bd.

3

Frederick the Great as Interpreted by Clausewitz and Schlieffen
Three Phases in the History of Strategy

In the early 1820s some years after he had begun writing *On War*, Clausewitz temporarily put the manuscript aside and wrote *The Campaigns of Frederick the Great from 1741 to 1762*.[1] To recognize the place that this historical study and the many others he wrote occupy in his work, it is necessary to go back through his life to the first years of his military service. In the eighteenth century men and women grew up quickly, and Clausewitz was only twelve when he joined the 34th Infantry as a lance-corporal, or officer aspirant, in 1792, the year Prussia entered the war against the new French Republic. After three years of active service in Alsace and on the Rhine he returned with his regiment to its barracks near Berlin. In the next decade, during which he was promoted first to ensign, then to lieutenant, he pieced together an education in service schools and study groups that extended beyond military matters to encompass philosophy, history, and literature. Still not twenty, he began to record his thoughts on the shifting conditions of Germany and Europe, and his reactions to the texts of the authors he was studying. Surviving papers from the next years refer to more than thirty authors, among them Frederick the Great and finally Jomini.[2]

At a time when much was being overturned, and to a generation that witnessed revolution at home and abroad, Jomini's belief that he had identified similarities in the operations of Frederick and Napoleon and was formulating what he claimed were strategic and operational principles of general validity was bound to be particularly seductive. Nor was Jomini the only one to seek a universally applicable strategic and operational system. Clausewitz, on the contrary, believed even as a junior officer that the wish for all-embracing formulae was misguided. The changing political and military environment showed him nothing that others did not see, but what he saw he saw differently. He, too, was concerned with the effective conduct of war under the new circumstances. He recognized, to mention only issues posed by his immediate environment, that the Frederician system, from manpower policy to tactics, had lost its supremacy—and years before the defeats of 1806 and 1807 drove the Prussian Army to adopt basic institutional and operational innovation, he developed views that later were to carry him into the ranks of the radical reformers. But effectiveness was not the only, nor even the ultimate goal of his military studies. Soon he wanted to understand the phenomenon of war as such. What little he knew of war in the past impressed him by the variety of methods applied to solve comparable issues, and in his mind he began to combine historical perspectives with perspectives of the present, joining the knowledge he could gain of wars in the past to his knowledge of war in the 1790s.

For some time philosophers and historians had been losing confidence in the Enlightenment's concept of abstract humanity progressing towards a more rational world. They were coming to appreciate the unique past of different cultures, each with individual characteristics that sought their own expression. Despite common features, modern societies differed; but such phenomena as politics or wars were general and shared by all. A basic identity existed between wars then and now, which made it possible to subject war to a structural analysis that rose above immediate issues. Whatever form manpower policy might take in the Prussian monarchy or the French republic, or had taken in the Roman Empire or in a tribe of aborigines, organizing men to fight was a universal and permanent element in history and of that part of history and current reality called war. Another type of constant element in war was the formation in which men fought. Tactics changed over time; but primitive or sophisticated, they always exist. Yet a third type of permanency was related not to policy but to the dynamics of hostile action and reaction, which could lead to an escalation of effort: escalation could potentially occur in a conflict between cavemen or between modern states.

The recognition that progress towards rationality was not the master key for understanding past and present, and that permanent elements in society and institutions could at any one time assume a variety of forms, nurtured Clausewitz's conception of war, towards which he began to feel his way before 1806: war as an entity made up of identifiable parts and processes, with its own dynamic, of opponents responding within a recognizable range of possibilities, the military potential and actions of each side linked to its political, social, economic, and cultural base. This last concept already points to Clausewitz's later formulation that war is the continuation of policy by other means, with which he identified not only attempts to achieve the aims of policy with organized violence, but also war as the expression of the political interests, pressures, and conflicts within the belligerent state—the German word *Politik* meaning both *policy* and *politics,* a dimension often ignored. As he was to write in *On War,* "Very few of the new manifestations in war [e.g., larger armed forces, which draw on all segments of the population] can be ascribed to new inventions or new departures in ideas. They result mainly from the transformation of society and new social conditions."[3] In the nuclear age he might qualify this statement, but would see no reason to withdraw it altogether: whatever the technological advances and their effects on society, it was society that used them.

An important step in the intellectual journey that Clausewitz began in these years was to write a political and military study of the campaigns of Gustavus Adolphus, probably in 1802, shortly before or soon after his twenty-second birthday, though not published until after his death, a work of some one hundred pages in print.[4] Clausewitz seems to have regarded discussing the Thirty Years' War and its historical interpretation as an opportunity to clarify his ideas on the nature of change as well as on the individuality of historical phenomena, both issues a general theory of war must accommodate. That he chose a subject that in Germany at the time was of literary rather than military interest is also an early sign of the cultural engagement that came to mark his entire work. Some years earlier, Schiller's *History of the Thirty Years' War* had made a strong impression on the educated public, as had his subsequent trilogy of dramas on Wallenstein, the Swedish king's great opponent. The last of the three plays, *Wallenstein's Death,* was given its first performance in Berlin as recently as 1799. In his correspondence Clausewitz cites Schiller more than once, both for his ethical idealism and for his dramatic power, and the poet's work remained a living force for him. Many years after he had written his account of Gustavus Adolphus, in December 1812 at the end of Napoleon's Russian campaign, when as a liaison officer with the Russians Clausewitz helped persuade the commander of the Prussian auxiliary corps, General Yorck, to disobey orders, quit the Grande Armée, and neutralize his force, he saw the conflict over loyalties with Schiller's eyes and compared the situation in which he found himself to the clash in *Wallenstein's Death* between officers who held firm to their general and others who planned to murder him.[5]

In his *History of the Thirty Years' War,* Schiller confronted the "emancipatory ambitions of his own time," its faith in reason and progress, "with the terrible past of the Thirty Years' War."[6] He interpreted the war as an "epoch of supreme national misery," from which great individuals, the heroes of his plays, nevertheless emerged. Less sympathetically, military opinion at the end of the eighteenth century dismissed the Thirty Years' War as three decades of primitive chaos and slaughter, now superseded by the rational warfare of the modern world. But, Clausewitz declared, that was to judge the seventeenth century with assumptions of a later time, and to misjudge the present as well. "Far from believing with some modern authors," he writes in the opening chapter of his study, "that the Thirty Years' War lasted so long because the generals did not know how to end it, we believe instead that modern wars have ended so quickly because men lacked the courage to defend themselves to the utmost"—a hidden reference to the failure in the 1790s of Great Britain and its German allies to halt the French revolutionary armies in Germany and the Low Countries, and incidentally a rejection of the claim that the past was inferior to the present. On the contrary, Clausewitz argues, in this case the present falls short.[7]

With Schiller he admired the great personalities of the period, but he went further and turned his admiration into an analytic principle and a critique of the rationalistic military concepts of the day—their effort to control war by turning it into a mathematical equation of physical forces that excluded the power of "moral, subjective" factors. "He who fails to study the heart and character of his enemy," he wrote, "will never decipher his decisions," an emphasis on psychology he was to repeat in *On War*.[8] He continued, that to understand the Thirty Years' War one must understand its particular material and intellectual conditions and the psychological makeup of its political and military leaders, which led to the unspoken conclusion that Gustavus Adolphus would not and could not wage war like Frederick the Great, just as Frederick could not be expected to fight like Napoleon. Like life, history demonstrated not only how human nature in its variety affected action, but also that a pattern of military action equally valid for the seventeenth, eighteenth, and nineteenth centuries did not exist. It was the task of a general theory of war to recognize the permanent elements of war and their interactions, and to recognize as well that the forms these components assumed were subject to constant change, which might demand always new responses: Theory should define the issues and actions of war, and explain what needed to be done, but not lay down laws on how to do it—for example, it should point out the need (and difficulty) of coordinating political goals and military action, but also that the desired coordination could be achieved in different ways.

In his search for an unbiased and undoctrinaire interpretation of the Thirty Years' War, Clausewitz follows methods that new directions in historical scholarship were then developing. His use of material is not yet systematic and he still relies wholly on printed sources, whether contemporary or published subsequently; but he strives not to interpret the past according to premises of his own day. And unlike some of the early practitioners of what might broadly be called historicism, who in their recognition of a culture's individuality easily fell in with the ideas, emotions, and language of the developing nation-state, he aims for objectivity and avoids ideology. Not only his studies of past wars, but those of wars in which he fought, are largely free of partisanship. He tries to be impartial—which does not signify scholarly remoteness. On the contrary, Clausewitz in his life as well as in his writings often undiplomatically revealed his feelings and political views in these years—the last years before

1806, during his service in that war in which he was taken prisoner, his return to Prussia in 1808, and his engagement in the efforts of reforming the army, culminating in rejecting his king's policies and imposing his own convictions by resigning from the Prussian service at the beginning of 1812, to avoid fighting for Napoleon in the invasion of Russia. But his insistence that Napoleon must be defeated never lessened his recognition of the emperor's genius, and his histories of the Russian invasion and of the final campaigns against Napoleon are remarkably evenhanded. His balanced approach was guided by the example of his fatherly friend Scharnhorst, whose dispassionate analysis in the 1790s of the reasons for the victories of the French revolutionary armies had helped give him an international reputation, and who had become the de facto leader of the military reform program. Clausewitz's objectivity was, however, more than following in the footsteps of an admired teacher. He had learned to see the unbiased view of the past as a precondition for the analysis of war as such.

During the years of intense intellectual and political activity after the defeat of 1806, theory was not in the forefront of Clausewitz's concerns. But even such a didactic task as his lectures in the War Academy on the "little war," the war of patrols and ambushes, lectures that introduced his students to a newly flexible tactical and operational system, includes observations on permanent issues that point to his mature theory—some reappear almost verbatim in *On War*.[9] From 1812 through the final campaigns against Napoleon to the first years of peace, he was able, despite his many duties first in Russian then again in Prussian uniform, to write accounts of the campaigns of 1812 and 1813. His return to Berlin in 1818 as director of the War Academy at last allowed him to divide his time between his duties and thinking and writing on matters not of immediate importance. Over the next thirteen years the politics of Restoration Europe drove him to write essays, both reflective and combative, on international politics and on the growing conflict between conservatives and liberals in Germany. When he began to write *On War* his expositions and arguments included many historical examples, a sign of the value he ascribed to history, and of his wish "to keep theory close to reality."[10] Not a few of his readers have misinterpreted these references to what had actually occurred as offering rules on future action, despite his declarations that it was not the task of theory to do so.[11] Frederick the Great and Napoleon are the historical figures most often cited in *On War*, and their wars the ones most often discussed. Other conflicts are also mentioned: wars in antiquity, and a larger number in the Middle Ages and the early modern period.[12] Many of these references, some brief, others longer, are drawn from or suggested by the historical studies he continued to write in an ongoing internal conversation between theory and history. One of these works is his study of *The Campaigns of Frederick the Great from 1741 to 1762*.

• • •

Shortly after his accession in 1740, Frederick had exploited the temporary policy uncertainties in the Austrian Empire after the death of Emperor Charles VI to occupy Silesia, a territorial addition that substantially strengthened Prussia and led to Austrian efforts in three wars, ending with the Seven Years' War, to recover the province. Much of the fighting in the three wars occurred over the same ground, and Clausewitz analyzed Frederick's operations in one continuous account, which he almost certainly wrote in the early 1820s. Since we can rarely determine just when a particular chapter of *On War* was written, the exact relationship between the two works can't be traced, but the many historical references in his theoretical work clearly show the connection with Clausewitz's historical studies. In some respects the history of Frederick is a counterpart of the history of Gustavus Adolphus, a work by a brilliant beginner, who now at the height of his analytic powers addresses the campaigns of the Prussian king. Both works are less operational narratives—major battles are often dealt with in a sentence or two—than strategic, political, and psychological analyses. As in his earlier study, Clausewitz pays attention to the psychology of the commanders, particularly of the commanders-in-chief: Gustavus Adolphus, and now Frederick, whose exceptional determination not to adjust his policies in the face of vastly superior force is turned from stubbornly embracing phantasies into a realistic sense of what may after all be possible by a strategy based on unremitting political calculations. In this opening chapter Clausewitz discusses the political nature of Frederick's campaigns, and of war in general. Never, he writes, "was strategy as suffused with politics as in this war" referring to the first two Silesian Wars as one.[13] His analytic survey of the leadership of both sides is closely linked to ideas we encounter again in his discussion in *On War* on the need to ensure that a war and its conduct are fully consonant with the political objectives. In *On War* he writes, "unless statesman and soldier are combined in one person, the only sound expedient is to make the commander-in-chief a member of the cabinet, so that the cabinet can share in the major aspects of his activities."[14] That was also the principal lesson of the three Silesian Wars, a lesson Clausewitz underlines by repeatedly noting the contrast between Frederick, the supreme political as well as military leader, facing alliances that had neither a commander-in-chief nor a supreme war council with significant authority. In each member of the alliance, moreover, political and military authority was divided, held by different individuals, who often had limited understanding of each other's situation and concerns. Finally, in the Seven Years' War, a powerful alliance was unable to defeat the much weaker Prussians in large part because more than once its members failed to coordinate force and policy, first in their own actions, and then with their allies, while Frederick understood and used the potential of politics and war as one. In the same way Clausewitz in his analytic reconstruction interprets the strategies and operations of the opposing sides by blending military and political aspects. What effect, he asks, is any particular action meant to create and does create in the opponent, his allies, in one's own allies, in public opinion? As an example he points to the fact that neither in the two first Silesian Wars nor in the Seven Years' War did Frederick attempt to occupy Vienna, an omission that Napoleon, for whom capital cities, the seats of government, were preferred targets, later called an error. But, Clausewitz writes, Frederick could not advance on Vienna without first neutralizing the main Austrian Army, an operation that he was too weak to risk. And even if he should succeed, how could he supply the long advance through hostile territory to Vienna? One must consider, Clausewitz continues, "the then existing realities ... Supplying the army in the manner usual since the French Revolution [i.e., by living off the land] was possible even then, but was not customary. It would have been taken as completely ravaging the country, and caused strong reactions in people's feelings and opinions."[15] The political consequences made a possibly desirable military operation unacceptable.

That seems an obvious conclusion, as obvious, one might think, as identifying war as the continuation of policy and politics by other means. But it is one thing to know and accept a self-evident truth, another to formulate it clearly, understand its place in theory, and apply it in practice. For an illustration, it may be useful to turn from the eighteenth to the twentieth century. In 1912, the retired chief of the German General Staff, Count Schlieffen, published *Frederick the Great*, a study of 126 pages of the king's wars, with a portfolio of 26 maps, as against Clausewitz's somewhat longer work on the same subject, published without maps. Schlieffen's study was reprinted the following year in his collected writings.[16] He was an accomplished interpreter of wars in history, even if he may have paid too much attention to their relevance to his own time.[17] His work on Frederick is based largely on the good, then recent biography by Koser, on extensive archival studies by the Historical Sections of the German General Staff, which gave him far more detailed information than Clausewitz had, and, oddly, on Carlyle's rather romantic biography of Frederick. In his history of Frederick, Schlieffen does not refer to Clausewitz; yet on the various issues of policy and strategy that Frederick faced in the three Silesian wars, which Schlieffen like Clausewitz treats as a continuous whole, he and Clausewitz largely agree. Clausewitz writes that after the opening campaigns, Frederick was always on the defensive; Schlieffen that Frederick fought what "basically was only a defensive war ... The task was difficult enough," he finds, and adds, thinking of the Napoleonic wars, that it "completely ruled out efforts to capture Vienna, Paris, or St. Petersburg."[18] But here we come to an important difference. Clausewitz declares that an army devastating the country as it advanced on Vienna would have created such a negative impact on public—that is, political—opinion that Frederick could not, and believed he could not, take the risk. Schlieffen, on the other hand, does not discuss the political dimension of the issue. He ignores it altogether.

That the political implications of a strategic decision were not uppermost in Schlieffen's mind is hardly surprising. From the time he was a cadet he had been taught that civilians and politicians must not interfere in military matters, an attitude favored by the constitutional arrangements of Imperial Germany. In his planning for a coming clash of Germany with France and Russia he left out of account the possible political consequences of a German envelopment of the French armies through Belgium (and in early versions of his plans also through the Netherlands), an idea not suggested to him, but illustrated by Hannibal's victory at Cannae in 216 BC, which he studied extensively. Schlieffen, writes the far from left-wing German historian Thomas Nipperdey, "neither included the political-ethical significance of the Belgian issue in his calculations, nor the military-political consequences of a British intervention ... the [German] military leadership demanded freedom from political considerations; but that," Nipperdey concludes, "in effect meant political supremacy."[19]

The publishing history of Schlieffen's *Frederick the Great* has an epilogue, which brings the problem of coordinating the political aim and military action, central for Clausewitz both in his history of Frederick and in *On War*, still closer to our own time. In 1927, Schlieffen's study was published for the third time, now as a separate volume with a foreword by General von Seeckt, the recently retired chief of the Army Command, the Reichswehr's senior officer, who in 1915 as General von Mackensen's chief of staff played a leading role in the German breakthrough in the Carpathian Mountains.[20] Like Schlieffen, Seeckt refers to Frederick's strategy—of which Clausewitz wrote that "never was strategy as infused with politics as in this war"—in purely military terms. A brief introduction cannot be expected to offer a comprehensive discussion, but Frederick's constant attention to the political factor in his strategic decisions should at least have been noted, and it is significant that Seeckt thought it either not necessary or not advisable to do so. During the difficult transition from Imperial Germany to Weimar Republic, Seeckt's position inevitably engaged him deeply in politics; but now, introducing Schlieffen's text, he wrote as if politics—once the decision to go to war was taken—had no place in a discussion of strategy and strategists. Instead he urges the reader to study Frederick and Schlieffen as examples of the supreme military leader, who is "made not by intelligence but by character," who has internalized "the strategic triad of time, space, and force," which leaves politics out of account, but is driven by "the absolute will to succeed"—a conception of supreme command that links technical expertise to romantic visions of "the power of the will," and one that Clausewitz would have regarded as both ridiculous and dangerously misleading.[21]

Clausewitz's historical studies expanded the reality on which his theories were based. They gave him the means to discuss war not only in its immediate manifestation, as a current or recent problem, but as an—until now—permanent part of the human condition, and one that at all times was a direct consequence of politics and political conditions. His history of Frederick recalls and explains a phase in the Prusso-German history of grand strategy, a phase in which political and military authority are closely linked, whether held by one man or by integrated authorities, and in which society, apart from small elites, is a relatively inert resource. Clausewitz himself, from the time the Prussian Army was reformed to the final campaigns against Napoleon and beyond, lived and wrote at the start of a second phase, in which effective authority remains centralized, but now also mobilizes and begins to shape broader social participation and emotions. At the onset of the nineteenth century," he notes in *On War*, "peoples themselves were in the scale on either side."[22] Schlieffen writes in a third phase, one that greatly expands the politically participatory public, fosters nationalism and patriotism that stimulate the new mass armies, and, it is hoped, help to discipline and control them, while the military leadership withdraws into professional isolation, and, as Seeckt's foreword indicates, prefers to judge political issues at home and abroad from a technical, purely military perspective, which, all courage and energy in army and society notwithstanding, led to Germany's defeat in the First World War. By then, Frederick's practical and Clausewitz's theoretical understanding of war as a continuation of policy and of politics, and the ability to apply that understanding, had been fatally weakened. What remained in a fourth and last phase in the history of strategy, which began with the National Socialist assumption of power in 1933, was technical proficiency, now coupled with the conduct of war as a murderous and suicidal continuation of ideology by other means.

Notes

1. Carl von Clausewitz, "Die Feldzüge Friedrichs des Grossen von 1741–62," in *Hinterlassene Werke*, X, Berlin, 1837, 29–254.
2. In 1808, soon after the publication of the first volumes of Jomini's *Traité de grande tactique*. For an overview of Clausewitz's life and studies during these years, see Eberhard Kessel's edition of Carl von Clausewitz, *Strategie aus dem Jahr 1804 mit Zusätzen von 1808 und 1809*, Hamburg, 1837, and my *Clausewitz and the State*, rev. ed., Princeton, 2007, 36–97.
3. Carl von Clausewitz, Book VI, ch. 30, *On War*, trans. and ed. Michael Howard and Peter Paret, Princeton, 1992, 45–46.
4. Carl von Clausewitz, "Gustav Adolphs Feldzüge von 1630–1632," in *Hinterlassene Werke*, IX, Berlin, 1837, 1–106.

5. Carl von Clausewitz, "Der Feldzug von 1812 in Russland," in *Hinterlassene Werke*, VII, Berlin, 1835, 227.
6. Walter Hinderer, *Schiller und kein Ende*, Würzburg, 2009, 244.
7. Carl von Clausewitz, "Gustav Adolphs Feldzüge von 1630-1632," in *Hinterlassene Werke*, IX, Berlin, 1837, 18.
8. Ibid., 8.
9. See the fifth essay in this work.
10. Carl von Clausewitz, "Author's Preface," *On War*, 61.
11. E.g. the section "Theory should be Study not Doctrine," Book II, ch. 2, ibid., 141.
12. Note, for example, the discussion of changes in war in Book VIII, ch. 3A, and the historical survey in Book VIII, ch. 3B of *On War*, 582-94.
13. Carl von Clausewitz, "Die Feldzüge Friedrichs des Grossen," *Hinterlassene Werke*, X, Berlin, 1837, 32
14. Carl von Clausewitz, Book VIII, ch. 6B, *On War*, 608
15. Carl von Clausewitz, "Die Feldzüge Friedrichs des Grossen" *Hinterlassene Werke*, X, Berlin, 1837, 4.
16. Alfred von Schlieffen, "Friedrich der Grosse," first published as a supplement to the *Vierteljahrshefte für Truppenführung und Heereskunde*, IX (1912), and reprinted in Alfred von Schlieffen, *Gesammelte Schriften*, Berlin, 1913, II, 19-149.
17. Note, for example, his comparisons between 1741 and 1900, ibid., 29, and between 1756 and 1870, ibid., 72.
18. Ibid., 141-42. Schlieffen valued Clausewitz as an inspiring example of the "thinking soldier." See his introduction to the fifth edition of *On War*, Berlin, 1905. Schlieffen's introduction was retained in the following ten editions of the work, including and up to the fifteenth edition, published in Berlin in 1937.
19. Thomas Nipperdey, *Deutsche Geschichte, 1866-1918*, Munich, 1992, II, 242.
20. Alfred von Schlieffen, *Friedrich der Grosse*, 2nd ed., Berlin, 1927. Seeckt's foreword was reprinted in several subsequent editions of Schlieffen's work.
21. Hans von Seeckt, ibid, unpaginated foreword.
22. Carl von Clausewitz, Book VIII, ch. 3A, *On War*, 583.

4

From Ideal to Ambiguity
Johannes von Müller, Clausewitz, and the People in Arms

In its efforts to break down legal divisions in society and extend participation in public affairs, the French Revolution took war out of the hands of a relatively restricted elite commanding long-serving professionals, and made it the business of the people. The integration of war and society proceeded along a number of ideological and institutional paths: careers were opened to talent; conscription—a more encompassing policy replacing already existing varieties of limited obligations to serve—was introduced, which brought previously protected men into the service; and civilians and soldiers were mobilized against domestic as well as foreign enemies, the so-called "people in arms," with its most dynamic expression, a general uprising—the *levée en masse*. Even before 1789 more than a few signs pointed in this direction. Rousseau discussed the individual's obligation to contribute to the common defense in a just society, and explicitly military proposals were advanced by such authors as Servan de Gerbey, the future Girondin minister of war, who in 1780 published a book with a title predicting what was to come, *Le Soldat-Citoyen*.

As international violence expanded, the debate on war grew more urgent. Its polite formulations cannot hide the intensity with which people sought to understand how war works with and against society. Among the many voices in this debate that deserve attention are two, coming from different directions, but both addressing the same central issue: the motivations of societies to go to war, which subsumes the further question as to the extent to which a country's inhabitants can be thought of as a political and moral entity. Quite apart from their particular arguments, the two speakers illuminate the general nature and tenor of the debate—a debate about war and its place in the world, which in different terms and with new urgency continues to this day. The two men express contrary ideas, but both use past events as stepping stones to conclusions about their own time. Consequently this summary of their views centers on two matters: their view of the demands and tasks of history as a discipline, and, secondly, their interpretation of war as a historical and contemporary phenomenon.

That one of the most widely read books on war in the last years before the French Revolution was a work of medieval history suggests the unmilitary character—in a technical sense—of much of the debate. In 1780 the young Swiss historian Johannes Müller published *Die Geschichten der Schweizer*, which, to evade the censor of Müller's hometown in northern Switzerland, Schaffhausen, listed Boston as the place of publication. His history of the Swiss, beginning in antiquity and ending with the Swiss victory over Leopold of Austria in the 1380s, made Müller a major figure in the scholarship and culture of his time. He developed a close relationship with Herder, Goethe took a friendly interest in his work to the point of translating his address on Frederick the Great at the Berlin Academy from the French original into German, while Schiller drew much of the material for his drama *Wilhelm Tell* from Müller's work. To repay his debt he added a reference to a fictitious character in his text: "Johannes Müller of Schaffhausen ... a man whose word can be trusted."[1] Müller became an important political publicist. His *Darstellung des Fürstenbundes* (1787) has been called the classic statement of the view that the Holy Roman Empire, an association of states and principalities with high degrees of autonomy, expressed a deeply rooted German appreciation for liberty.[2] He served in the administration of a number of German states, was raised to the nobility in the Electorate of Mainz, became the royal historiographer of the Prussian monarchy, and continued work on his Swiss history to the end of the fifteenth century.[3] After Prussia's defeat in the War of 1806 and the French occupation of Berlin, he entered the service of Jerome Bonaparte, a step patriotic German historians of the nineteenth and twentieth centuries found unforgiveable. He died in 1809 as head of the department of education of the new Napoleonic kingdom of Westphalia.[4]

Although the only translation of his book during his lifetime was an unauthorized, bad English version, Müller's fame spread beyond Central Europe. Mme. de Staël in *De l'Allemagne* singled him out among German historians.[5] In 1806 her great enemy Napoleon found it worth his while to discuss history and politics with Müller for more than an hour, during which he urged him to bring his Swiss history forward to the present. Their meeting ended with the emperor and his guest attending a concert, which as a mark of imperial courtesy included compositions on Swiss themes.

What was it that gave Müller's work international resonance? The subject of medieval peasants combining to gain and defend their independence certainly responded to the Enlightenment's fascination with the goodness and strength of an unspoiled people and to the philosophical appeal of freedom. It also spoke to doubts as to the fate of freedom in the real world as a new nation was emerging in America, but Poland was partitioned and external pressures and domestic conflicts threatened Swiss independence itself. One objective of Müller's work was to contrast political freedom with absolutism and to interpret the early history of the Swiss as the expression of universal forces, an idea associated with his interest in world history. A second motive was to recall the modern Swiss to the virtue and political sagacity of their ancestors. I wish, Müller informed his readers, "to depict the old confederation in such vigorous colors that you can compare its periods and requirements with our own, and determine the efforts and wisdom that are necessary to prove ourselves worthy descendants of such forefathers, and continue their work."[6] For Müller, writing his book was not only a profoundly emotional exploration of the Swiss past, but a political assertion.

He made this act more effective and broadened its appeal with a text in which he recreated the past with great specificity, even as he gave it contemporary meaning. Much of his work's strength lies in its style, which, though not elegant, was capable of treating the widest range of subjects with unflagging attention and interest, from social customs of the rural population and the complex relationships in and between leading aristocratic dynasties to town charters and the military practices of the Swiss and their various opponents. Friedrich Gundolf, partly in recognition of Müller's literary powers, called him Ranke's "most immediate and greatest predecessor;"[7] while Felix Gilbert placed Müller among historians who are "great writers," and whose style enters into the substance of their interpretations.[8] A notable characteristic of Müller's text is the close interaction of great specificity with emotional appeals to the reader. His engagement with the sources, many of which he was the first to bring to light from local and family archives, lent even his dramatic effusions an odd archival solidity. Müller's documentation is unusually extensive for his time—and, indeed, for ours: thirty pages, listing manuscripts and printed sources, preceding the 444 pages of text of the 1780 edition. This mass of material is enriched by sources of another kind—references to the Swiss climate, geography, and economy—from which, following Montesquieu, Müller deduced the peoples' *esprit général*. To discover the manners of the ancient Swiss he explored villages in remote valleys and searched legends and songs for clues to earlier attitudes, a line of interpretation fed by the works of such Swiss writers as Haller, Lavater, and Bodmer, whose celebration of the Swiss and their past foreshadow a later romantic glorification of "the people," and from whose poems he chose epigraphs to signal the purpose of his work:

> Tell us, Helvetia, you homeland of heroes!
> How do your ancients relate to your people today?

and

Brothers know your strength: it is loyalty.
If only loyalty were reawakened in every reader!

Müller's use of sources has been questioned. Among much else he has been criticized for exaggerating the extent of political participation in the old Swiss communities, and modern sociological analysis has corrected generalizations about the medieval peasant that he adopted and reinforced; inevitably his work has been superseded. Friedrich Meinecke even dismisses his histories altogether: they are not like "a spring of fresh water," he writes, " but ... a sponge that soaked up many liquids—namely, tendencies of the age—and squeezed them out again."[9] This rejection at least recognizes Müller's value as a witness and historical source.

Two ideas, one political, the other on war, underlie Müller's work. The history of the Swiss, he says, was shaped by the common man's demand for freedom from alien rule. This agrees with popular myth, which identifies the founders of the Swiss confederation as "pious, noble peasants." Müller's narrative and documentation gives these populist claims new weight. To his German readers living under absolutist governments he holds up the confederation as a latter-day version of Greek democracy, which they could prize as a cultural ideal, if not as an end to strive for. His concept of democracy, it should be said, was decidedly aristocratic. He valued the Swiss past, as he saw it, but accepted the domination of local elites and did not find it inconsistent in his book on Swiss freedom to declare Frederick the Great the paragon of modern rulers.[10]

The second—military—thesis of Müller's book combines the idealism of the Swiss with their courage and their love of war. The Swiss, Müller repeatedly states, were innately and to an exceptional degree warlike. It was this deep-seated attitude that turned the people's love of freedom into a historical force. His book, an early example of military history in which the main actor is the common fighting man, celebrates war as the prerequisite of freedom, and the medieval Swiss as the champions of both. "Only iron and steel," he declares in a typical passage, "keep a state free."[11] Similar expressions—"the militia is the most essential part of society ... The warlike spirit is our lifeblood"—occur throughout the book, which concludes in a paragraph (incidentally, a good example of Müller's style) that sums up its author's view that the armed citizen, imbued with the ideal of freedom, stands at the center of the free and just community: "We have seen as united people," Müller writes, "overcome ignorant knights and their followers, exploit the mountain passes, yet rely not only on the mountains but also on themselves; become warriors of freedom, the more warlike the freer, and prove repeatedly that military virtue can make up for much else, and that without this virtue statecraft means nothing."[12] These words once more universalize the Swiss experience, and in the era of late absolutism with its long-serving mercenaries are doubly revolutionary in their exaltation of the citizen-soldier. Müller's book depicts the medieval Swiss as a "people in arms," in what might be called the concept's idealized, "natural" condition, not in the organized version the French Revolution was soon to introduce.

An issue in Swiss history Müller faces indirectly if at all is the gradual change from coming together for the common defense to aggressive policies. Unifying the cantons entailed seizing territories in feudal dependence on more than one authority or with significant non-Swiss populations. To defend access to the outer Swiss rim, it was desirable to occupy areas far from the original cantons. In the period treated in Müller's first book, these accessions were limited; but by the fifteenth century, which his later writings covered, Swiss expansion to the west and in Italy contributed to destabilizing the region. At this time, in the words of the official Swiss military history published during the First World War, "the Confederation reveal[ed] a new military and political posture. The struggle for independence is past. Individual cantons or alliances of cantons now seek to expand their territory in all directions."[13]

Expansion was not necessarily aggression. Frequently it filled a vacuum or reacted to external political or military pressure. Müller carefully traces these various conflicts. An example is his reconstruction of the diplomatic and military operations in the 1420s to retain the earlier Swiss conquest of Bellinzona at the edge of the Lombard plain. He cites a cantonal representative at a meeting of the various cantons to decide on the extent, if any, of their armed participation in this campaign, who concedes that "Bellinzona is not part of the confederation. But it is natural and necessary," he continued, "that these territories remain Swiss. We have the right to rule up to the line where the mountain range becomes the Lombard plain, because these strong passes cannot be occupied by the enemy without placing us in manifold dangers."[14] Müller discusses the motives and disagreements of the various cantons, and analyzes the "party spirit," which he holds responsible for lack of cohesive action and identifies as a weakness that is beginning to affect the confederation as a whole. But he fails to turn the shift from fighting for independence to fighting for expansion—if often with defensive motives—into a major theme in the history of the confederation, a theme, one may think, of comparable significance to that of the long struggle for autonomy, which he had interpreted as the expression of Swiss combative idealism.

The united cantons had grown into a great military power—for several generations Swiss military organization and tactics were the most effective in Europe—and the confederation showed no signs of limiting its energies to defense however generously defined, until severe defeats revealed that it had overreached itself, a recognition that eventually led to a policy of permanent neutrality. Earlier two related forces had been at work, the export of fighting men to other states and conquest, whether motivated by the wish for security or greed, neither of which fit the ideal of the freedom-loving citizen-warrior. Müller addresses the rise of the Swiss mercenary, which confirmed his belief in the Swiss people's warlike nature, and distinguishes the policies by which the cantons supplied troops to foreign princes from the willingness of men, often driven by lack of work, to seek service abroad.[15] But he cannot fully recognize, let alone reconcile, the aggressiveness that the confederation and its people now revealed, with the "noble, pure herdsman-warrior" of legend, to which his writings had given new credence. He seems not to have realized that the Swiss pursuit of conquest as well as of freedom called his basic thesis of the people's pure political ethics into question.

A solution to this contradiction is offered by the second speaker here singled out in the late Enlightenment debate on the motivation of societies to go to war, Carl von Clausewitz. As a young man, born the year Müller published the first volume of his history, Clausewitz in 1804 came to know its author, who had recently arrived in Berlin. Both men belonged to a circle whose senior members two years later, as Napoleon was preparing to attack Prussia, called on Frederick William III, in a memorial Müller drafted, to meet the crisis by modernizing the government and strengthening its links with the people—unasked advice the king indignantly rejected.[16]

After Prussia's defeat in 1806 and 1807, Clausewitz's egalitarian and functional modernism drove him toward the most activist reformers, some of whom in the years before Napoleon's Russian campaign thought seriously about a Prussian version of the people in arms. Then and later the king and conservative advisors suspected Clausewitz of being politically unreliable, if not a Prussian Jacobin, a reputation that was to affect his career in years to come.[17]

As the young Clausewitz's interest in the wars of his own day expanded to the history of war and the study of war as such, he began to write papers and soon several long studies on war in the past. His notebooks of 1804 include several pages on the medieval Swiss, which are based on the work of Johannes von Müller.[18] Clausewitz's notes discuss *how* the Swiss fought, not *why*, and do not address Müller's idealization of the Swiss people in arms. In other notes of the time and in his later writings he rejects interpretations that are one-dimensional; here he merely refers to a statement by Müller—borrowed, he observes, from Machiavelli—that before the introduction of firearms, underdeveloped and isolated societies like the Swiss were better at fighting than societies with rich and sophisticated military cultures, which seems to deny the uniqueness of the Swiss.

A comparison of Clausewitz's ideas with Müller's should begin by noting a basic difference between them: the study of the past and writing about it were one man's principal concern, while the other saw the analysis of war in the past as the essential prerequisite for arriving at an understanding of war itself. As the comparison is continued, it reveals the characteristics of Clausewitz's approach to history and how it differs from that of Müller with particular clarity. In his reliance on a small body of published sources he is far more traditional. On the other hand, he does not write partisan history. He tries not to judge the past by the ideals and concerns of his own day, and Müller's moralizing assumptions of late-Enlightenment historiography are alien to him. Clausewitz's historical writings, as distinct from some of his commentary in the first shock after Prussia's defeat in 1806, are rarely skewed by such factors as national identity, social allegiance, or political ideology. He combines the effort to put himself in the place of the people he writes about with a critical analysis of their ideas and actions.

Clausewitz's theoretical works, their arguments and conclusions, are replete with references to historical events and their interpretation. He never outlined his views of historical methodology fully and definitively, but he often reflects on these matters in his writings.[19] An extended example is the third chapter, "Critical Analysis" of Book II of *On War*, in which he contrasts the plain narrative of an event with what he calls the critical approach, consisting in "the discovery and interpretation of equivocal facts, the tracing of effects back to their causes, and the investigation and evaluation of the means employed."[20] If objectivity in narrating an event and in its critical analysis was an ideal for Clausewitz, it was also a necessity, because his interest in history, though central to his thinking, was in the first instance driven by his wish to understand not a particular war or the wars of his generation, but war as a constant in history. Causes and attitudes mattered and had to be studied, but much of war proceeded apart from them, and the basic elements of employing and fending off armed force had to be understood before adding motives to armed action and reaction in specific cases. To distinguish the particular from the general, to identify the permanent elements in war and understand their adjustment to technological, political, and social change, Clausewitz needed to make comparisons over time as objectively as he could. He began with the Frederician, post-Frederician, and Napoleonic eras, the French Revolution forming the great divide. Later he extended his range over European history from the Middle Ages to the beginnings of the Industrial Revolution, with an occasional glance at antiquity. His treatment of Napoleon is a good example of the analytic detachment he aimed for, and that he achieved to a degree sufficient to make possible realistic comparisons between wars of the seventeenth, eighteenth, and early nineteenth centuries even as he noted the individuality of the various periods. Since the comparative method was an essential element in the analytic process with which Clausewitz developed his theories, its application had to be as unaffected as possible by cultural and ideological preconceptions, including his own.

This way of thinking about the past is already evident in his first extended study, written in his early twenties, at the latest when he was twenty-five, in which he rejects the Enlightenment's view of the Thirty Years' War as a chaotic muddle and instead explains its drawn-out operations with the economy and technology of the age, the social characteristics of the troops, and the commanders' politics and not least their psychology—a declaration of intellectual independence that signals the audacity of his approach to the past.[21] From then on, Clausewitz's attention to psychological factors became part of and emphasized the compound character of his interpretations of history, as of the present. His concern to maintain objectivity may make it unnecessary to add that he avoided any partisanship in his treatment of religious antagonisms in the Thirty Years' War or of its various conflicts between Germans and French, Swedes, or Danes, and between Germans themselves.

A subsequent example of this detachment appears in the beginning of *On War*. The work addresses its subject as the sum of decisions, actions, and reactions in an uncertain, dangerous context, but also as a sociopolitical phenomenon. The opening chapter offers several definitions as analytic starting points, the most widely cited identifying war as the continuation of politics or policy by other means. The chapter ends with yet another definition, which encompasses both the sociopolitical and the operational: the tripartite nature of war.

As a total phenomenon, Clausewitz writes, war is a remarkable trinity. It is composed of passion and violence, of chance and probability, and of its "element of subordination, as an instrument of policy." To give these abstractions greater meaning he links each to a tangible reality. Violence, which he regards as "a blind, natural instinct," is primarily associated with the people; chance and probability, which give scope to the creative spirit, are mainly the concern of the commander and the army. The subordination of war to political decisions relates to "the government"—by which Clausewitz means the political leadership, whether of a migratory tribe or a modern state.[22]

This is not the only part of the tripartite definition in which Clausewitz's choice of words may be open to misunderstanding. He also leaves uncertain whether by "the people" he refers to the subordinate mass, or a totality encompassing both commoners and elites—"the German people" or "the Swiss people." His historical writings, however, indicate that he means the people as a whole. He attributes the Napoleonic Wars, to give one example, to the emperor's compulsions and calculations, not to any particular propensity for war on the part of the French.[23] But—and this is his point—Napoleon would have failed sooner had not the French, like other societies, accepted violence and been prepared to use it. Imposing this universal on the history of the Swiss leads Clausewitz to conclude that they liked to fight and were good at it, whether for freedom, pay, or conquest—all significant motives, none of which negates the others.

Müller writes of the Swiss "joy in war" or "eagerness for war" (*Kriegslust*),[24] a concept some later historians changed to "craving or addiction for war" (*Kriegssucht*); but he dignifies their pleasure by placing it in the service of freedom.

When the Swiss turn aggressive, their historian falls silent. Against Müller's reductive idealization of his people as driven by a single or at the very least by a defining, dominant cause, Clausewitz asserts the ambiguities of multifaceted realism. The medieval Swiss, he suggests in his note of 1804, were neither more nor less warlike than other largely rural societies at the time, and—we may extrapolate from his tripartite definition—they could be motivated, like everyone else, by more than one cause or interest, held simultaneously or in succession, all resting on the ready and natural acceptance of violence: the Swiss, fighting for freedom in the Alps, also fight for conquest in the Lombard plains. During the French Revolution Europe experienced a comparable shift, when the French first defended their country against invasion, after which they exploited their successful defense by launching aggressive wars that led to their occupying much of the continent. By joining other Swiss writers in celebrating the Swiss people, which prefigures a common romantic theme, and by not analyzing the shift from defending their independence to expanding their territory but instead allowing himself the politically desirable idealization of the old Helvetians, Müller weakens his book, perhaps not as an ethical or political statement, but as history.

Müller and Clausewitz were early participants in the discussion of war and society, at a time when the expansion of war raised new intellectual, political, and moral problems for Europe, and soon for the rest of the world. In this debate, the question of the extent to which the medieval Swiss fought for an ideal, for self-interest, or out of a ready acceptance of violence as a political instrument stands for the larger question of why men fight at all, which goes to the very nature of war itself.

Müller's idealization of the people in arms and Clausewitz's differentiated alternative may have been influenced by the fact that one man wrote before, the other after the civil violence and the terror of the French Revolution. But the difference also reflects their personalities, their motives, and the bent of their minds: Müller, whom Goethe with his eye for the essential praised for the enthusiasm of his work, and Clausewitz, his seemingly detached, analytical counterpart. If for an instant we extend their ideas to contemporary politics, we find that neither man can be accurately labelled "liberal" or "conservative," whether in his time or today. Müller's hopeful view of the autonomous people as a force for good, even for peace—an assumption that made its appearance in the literature of the later Enlightenment—belongs to the rhetoric of any modern nation-state, whether democratic or not, prone to war or peaceful. At the same time, his assertion, "Only iron and steel can keep a state free ... the warlike spirit is our lifeblood ... without [military] virtue statecraft means nothing," could as well have been written by Bismarck.

Clausewitz presents a more complex case. Ironically for this proponent of change in Prussia, his skeptical realism, and his tripartite definition that ambiguously links violence to the people, may convey a conservative political message. On the other hand, although before the First World War official German Army histories minimized the radicalism of the Prussian reform era, German military critics of Clausewitz before 1914 were troubled by many of his ideas—not least that, as his tripartite definition declares, military action should be subordinate to political authority because in the last analysis it is political not military success that matters in war. Yet they never objected to his attributing violence, passion, and the irrational to the undefined people at large.

If for a moment we leave the politics of the two men to one side, turn from any subsequent political implications of their writings to their way of posing and analyzing issues, and take note of their intellectual style, we may find that Müller's sense of the people as a unitary force and Clausewitz's pragmatic probing of this concept offer a preview of the clash between liberals and conservatives that defined the political history of nineteenth-century Europe, strongly marked the historiography of the time, and shaped its military institutions. Progressive parties, even those not yet prepared to support universal suffrage, drew great energy from rhetorically elevating the people to stand for all that is good in public life. In contrast, their conservative enemies' questioning of this ideal, and their practice of pointing to the self-interest and ambiguous motives of factions and groups, gave adherents of government by elites a tactical advantage that enabled them to fight rearguard actions, often with considerable success, well into the twentieth century. Conservatives, to be sure, developed their own sacred unities, or adopted them from the left—"the nation" for instance—and filled them with their very different values.

The debate in which Müller and Clausewitz were early participants, at times concurring, but basically disagreeing, continues. Both knew that to penetrate to the core of their subject meant looking beyond its immediate borders. Müller makes war a major element in his study of medieval Swiss society and of the emergence of a Swiss political culture, which retains its major characteristics over centuries. Clausewitz analyzes war—its purpose and function as well as its methods—on the basis of the social, cultural, and political forces from which the resort to organized violence emerges. Each man saw and interpreted his subject in the round, an approach as valuable and as difficult to implement today as it was two centuries ago. Müller combined his comprehensive view of the Swiss past with its idealization, a celebration that may have contributed to the very favorable reception his work enjoyed for years—elevating one's native soil when writing its history seemed and seems natural and appropriate to many. What Müller did in his history of the Swiss, others—either already in agreement with him or learning from his example—would attempt when it came to trace the events and values of their own people. Occasionally, this tendency moved from the writing of history, whether of a people, a period, or a war, to the theoretical understanding of war—not as war was conducted by a particular country or state, but to the nature of armed conflict itself. A striking example of this shift is the theoretical work of a Prussian officer whose career was for long, and often closely, associated with Clausewitz's life and work: Rühle von Lilienstern, who placed an ethical standard—which he located in the concept of defensive war—at the center of his theories, an extension that instead of strengthening his arguments filled them with contradictions, and that foretold generations of confused reactions to Clausewitz's attempt to understand war as it actually is.[25]

Clausewitz's response to Müller's histories of the Swiss is an early step in his reading and thinking about history, and soon in his writing about history as well—activities that quickly begin to exert an influence on his first conceptualizations of war as such. Focused on the past and focusing on the present and future combine in his mind. He learns from the discussion of social, institutional, and political specifics, and soon accepts their relevance to the understanding of war. But he is careful about attributing absolute authority to "higher values," even to those that are his own. They may indeed exist, but usually are resisted by opponents equally convinced of the ethical validity of *their* beliefs. He accepts the strengths and limitations of French as well as of German patriotism—a differentiated view that not only energizes his historical interpretations, but also keeps his theories free of easily misleading partisan encumbrances. Müller's emphasis on the ethical as the formative force in the history of the Swiss has no equal either in Clausewitz's histories or in his theories. First as a historian, soon as a theorist, Clausewitz shows himself unwilling to accept the central place of idealism in Müller's work. Instead he tries to recognize ambiguous reality. In his study of history he distinguishes between good and bad as he perceives them to be, between the creative and the stultifying, and acknowledges the far-reaching effect each may have; but in the theory of war, in his analysis of the interaction of the various elements, large and small, that make up war from its inception to its conclusion and consequences, the ethical, however defined and often seen very differently from different perspectives, is to him not a dominant force. He sees it instead as merely one element of historical energy among many that a theory of war must accommodate.

Notes

1. Friedrich von Schiller, *Wilhelm Tell*, Act 5, Scene 1.
2. Klaus Epstein, *The Genesis of German Conservatism*, Princeton, 1966, 253, n 25.
3. Johannes von Müller, *Geschichten Schweizerischer Eidgenossenschaft*, rev. ed., vols. I–V, Leipzig, 1825–1826, originally published 1786–1808.
4. The literature on Müller's life is substantial. Three standard works are: Edgar Bonjour, *Studien zu Johannes von Müller*, Basel, c. 1957; Karl Schib, *Johannes von Müller*, Schaffhausen-Konstanz, 1967; and the collection of essays, edited by Christoph Jamme

and Otto Pöggeler, *Johannes von Müller—Geschichtsschreiber der Goethezeit*, Schaffhausen, 1986.
5. Anne-Louise-Germaine de Staël, "Des historiens allemands, et de J. De Müller en particulier," *De l'Allemagne*, Paris, 1810, part 2, ch. 6.
6. Johannes von Müller, "Vorwort," *Geschichten Schweizerischer Eidgenossenschaft*, I, xxxviii.
7. Friedrich Gundolf, *Anfänge Deutscher Geschichtsschreibung*, Amsterdam, 1938, 4.
8. Felix Gilbert, *History: Politics or Culture?* Princeton, 1990, 99. See also, ibid., 14.
9. Friedrich Meinecke, *Die Entstehung des Historismus*, Munich, 1946, 309.
10. Johannes Müller, "Vorrede," *Die Geschichten der Schweizer*, Boston [Schaffhausen], 1780, v–xxi.
11. Ibid., 153.
12. Ibid., 444.
13. R. von Fischer, "Die Feldzüge der Eidgenossen diesseits der Alpen…," *Schweizer Kriegsgeschichte*, ed. M. Feldmann and H. G. Witz, Bern, 1915, I, part 2, 53.
14. Müller, *Geschichten Schweizerischer Eidgenossenschaft*, III, 191.
15. Ibid., I, 113.
16. In his account of Prussian conditions before the reforms, which was so critical that it could not be included in his collected works, Clausewitz refers to the memorial, written by "the famous historian Johannes von Müller," *Nachrichten über Preussen in seiner grossen Katastrophe; Kriegsgeschichtliche Einzelschriften*, Berlin, 1888, X, 440. See also the sixth essay in the present work, and my *Clausewitz and the State*, rev. ed., Princeton, 1985, 113–17.
17. The most overt episode occurred in 1819, when the Prussian minister of foreign affairs proposed Clausewitz as ambassador to the Court of St. James. The appointment was not made, according to the British envoy to Berlin, because the king and his advisors feared that Clausewitz was not free of revolutionary tendencies. See my "Bemerkungen zu dem Versuch von Clausewitz zum Gesandten in London ernannt zu werden," *Jahrbuch für die Geschichte Mittel- und Ostdeutschlands* 26 (1977), and the later editions of my *Clausewitz and the State*.
18. Carl von Clausewitz, "6. Geist der Kriegskunst bei den Schweizern," *Strategie aus dem Jahr 1804, mit Zusätzen von 1808 und 1809*, ed. Eberhard Kessel, Hamburg, 1937, 43–44. Kessel published the main body of notes, together with an important introduction. Some additional notes were published by Walter Schering in his blatantly National-Socialist edition of Clausewitz's writings *Geist und Tat*, Stuttgart, 1941.
19. See Hans Delbrück, "General von Clausewitz," in *Historische und politische Aufsätze*, Berlin, 1887; Hans Rothfels, *Carl von Clausewitz: Politik und Krieg*, Berlin, 1920, reprinted Bonn, 1980; Eberhard Kessel's introduction to the work is cited in footnote 18 above; Paret, *Clausewitz and the State*, chapters 5 and 11, part ii, and "Introduction to Part One," in Carl von Clausewitz, *Historical and Political Writings*, ed. and trans. Peter Paret and Daniel Moran, Princeton, 1992.
20. Carl von Clausewitz, *On War*, ed. and trans. Michael Howard and Peter Paret, Princeton, 1976, 156.
21. Carl von Clausewitz, "Gustav Adolphs Feldzüge von 1630–1632," in *Hinterlassene Werke des Generals Carl von Clausewitz über Krieg und Kriegführung*, Berlin, 1837, IX.
22. Clausewitz, "What Is War?" *On War*, Book 1, ch. 1, 89. On the trinity, see also the discussion in the first essay of the present work.
23. This was Clausewitz's opinion even during the emotionally charged period when he was a prisoner of war in France. After seeing police officers lead shackled conscripts to the prefecture, he commented that although this "shameful procedure" demonstrates

the government's "extreme military tendencies…, there is no trace of these in the character of the nation." Journal entry of 25 August 1807, Karl Schwarz, *Leben des Generals Carl von Clausewitz…*, Berlin, 1878, I, 107–8.
24. E.g., Müller, *Geschichten Schweizerischer Eidgenossenschaft*, III, 21, n. 34.
25. On Rühle, his theories and his misinterpretations of *On War,* see the second essay of the present work.

5

"Half against My Will, I Have Become a Professor"

After its defeat in the War of 1806 the Prussian Army underwent far-reaching reforms, as part of which the system of military education was restructured and expanded. Some of the major decisions concerning the army's reorganization were already being implemented when an order of 2 May 1810 determined the new organization of the cadet institutes, established three military schools for ensigns, and founded an academy for "officers qualified for advanced instruction."[1] Even after French pressure compelled Scharnhorst, the man at the center of the reform efforts, to resign as head of the General War Department, in effect the Ministry of War, he remained director of military education, and arranged for two of his most trusted subordinates to serve as instructors at the new War Academy : Carl von Tiedemann to lecture on strategy and tactics, Carl von Clausewitz to give the course on the Little War (*Kleiner Krieg* = *petite guerre*, war of outposts, patrols, etc.). To his friend August Neidhardt von Gneisenau, the future field marshal, Clausewitz wrote, "Half against my will, I have become a professor."[2] That at the beginning of its existence the academy—then called the General War School (Allgemeine Kriegsschule)—had gained two gifted teachers with broad combat experience, who early on had recognized the weaknesses of the old system, lent the school intellectual heft, and held out promise for the future. Did their teaching the two courses exert a comparably large influence on the further development of Tiedemann's and Clausewitz's thinking?

In Tiedemann's case, his early death voids the question. After Prussia's forced alliance with France in February 1812, he resigned his commission, left Prussia to join the Russian Army, and in August was killed as chief of staff of the Russian forces defending Riga against Macdonald's 10th corps of the Grande Armée. Clausewitz also quit the Prussian Army and took service in Russia, but survived, and in the progression of his thoughts on war the lectures play a role—as a test of his views on the nature, possibilities, and limitations of theory, and as a link between early and later ideas in the long succession of his writings.

The part his lectures played in these developments is more clearly recognized when the lectures are considered in their different aspects: in their place in Clausewitz's biography, their purpose and method, and in their links to the reforms as a whole on the one hand and to Clausewitz's later writings on the other. Each of these themes deserves to be treated comprehensively; here I must limit myself to identify and summarize their essential elements.

In 1810, Prussia, much reduced in territory, was a satellite in the Napoleonic Empire, carefully watched, but at the same time intensively and partly in secret modernizing its government, administration, and army. Despite their often conflicting views, the supporters of reform had learned to work together. They were driven by a belief that Napoleon was overextending himself, and that a new war could lead to the restoration of the state's independence. Although their plans and innovations encountered considerable resistance among conservative elites in army and country, they achieved many though not all of their goals. For Clausewitz these demanding years were a successful, happy period. In December 1810, after an engagement of four years, he married Marie von Brühl. His work as Scharnhorst's closest assistant gave him insight into the interaction, both collaborative and conflicting, between politics, society, and the army. At the age of thirty a major on the General Staff, teacher at the War Academy, and tutor in the military sciences to the crown prince and two other members of the royal family, he could look forward to a good, even brilliant career, until in 1812 when he quit Prussia to avoid having to fight for Napoleon. Clausewitz's decision troubled and offended the king, who may even have felt it to be an act of disobedience, and his sense of unease over Clausewitz's independence and willfulness was never to dissipate entirely.

Among Clausewitz's various duties in the years before he left Prussia, two best enabled him to combine his ideas on the particulars of the army's reforms with his thinking on the basic elements, processes, and dynamics of war as such: his tutorials, which were far-reaching and generalized, and his lectures on the Little War, which were specific and intensely detailed. Since Werner Hahlweg edited Clausewitz's manuscript of the lectures and in 1966 published it with an introduction and extensive commentary, we possess an accurate text.[3] Professor Hahlweg's reconstruction is merely one among his many publications of Clausewitz's manuscripts and of his own bibliographical and historical studies, which puts every student of Clausewitz's work in his debt. That does not mean that one must agree with every one of his interpretations. This essay will propose a reading of Clausewitz's lectures that in several respects diverges from Professor Hahlweg's views.

Clausewitz lectured on the Little War from 15 October 1810 to the end of June of the following year, four hours a week, for a total of 156 hours. He repeated the course with some changes and new material from October 1811 until the course was broken off in April 1812 when he resigned his commission. The manuscript of the lectures comprises 230 pages in print.[4] In his introductory remarks Clausewitz announces that Tiedemann's lectures on tactics will "treat the nature of war in its main outlines"—a statement that, as it practically equates tactics with the "nature of war," points to the high significance of the change from the old to a new tactical system in Prussia. He himself, Clausewitz continues, will talk about "the entire outpost system and other security measures of the army, as well as the actions of smaller groups with offensive goals," and the staff measures linked to it, meaning reconnaissance, operational decisions, and similar matters. The two courses would be closely coordinated.[5] After these introductory remarks, Clausewitz turns to the subject of his first lecture, "Introduction to the Little War," which he begins with three questions: "What is the little war?" "What makes it a separate field of study?" and "How does [the teaching of the Little War] fit in with other military instruction?"

Clausewitz's answer to these questions reflects the approach and tone of his lectures overall, and is worth giving at length: "With the term Little War," he begins, "we understand the employment of small detachments in the field. Actions of 20, 50, 100, or 300 to 400 men belong to the Little War, if they are not part of a larger engagement." This definition, he continues, "may seem mechanical and unscientific, but if we keep the current use of the term 'Little War' in mind it is correct, perhaps it is even the only possible definition—although to demonstrate that would lead us too far afield. In short, all military actions of small units are objects of the Little War. Of course," he continues, "we can't strictly determine what we mean by small and large units; nor is that necessary here. Many other definitions do not precisely separate large and small, and are nevertheless neither wrong nor meaningless. It is sufficient that we explain our reason for defining matters in this way."[6]

These opening sentences already express an attitude familiar from other of Clausewitz's writings: the rejection of strict, absolute definitions, a denial that is linked with the author's skepticism about applying rules and laws to a subject as dynamic and dominated by opposing, antagonistic interests and actions as war. Regulations are valid for technical particulars. One can follow them, he says, in establishing or striking a camp; but war is not a mechanical construct that functions according to firm rules. In *On War* Clausewitz rejects rules that demand absolute authority as abstractions, "bookish rules" not valid in the real world. "The art of war," he writes, "deals with living and with moral forces. Consequently it cannot attain the absolute, or certainty."[7] The explanation he gives in his opening lecture implies that it is the task of the theorist and, up to a point, of the instructor, to recognize the essence and purpose of the various elements that together make up the conduct of war. If the identity of the Little War lies in the fact that it is conducted by forces of relatively small size acting with a degree of independence as agents of a larger force, a more abstract definition would not only be unnecessary but misleading.

It may be assumed that Clausewitz's freely ranging introductory outline, rising above the claimed precision and authority of a prescriptive definition, had a liberating effect on many of his students. Others may have been troubled by the lack of rules, which foretold the new degree of flexibility that characterizes the lectures as a whole. Judging from the generally effective performance of the reconstituted army in the campaigns from 1813 to 1815, the new tactical doctrine to which Clausewitz's lectures pointed was on the whole employed successfully, with even the grenadier battalions, the infantry units of greatest solidity and power, gaining a new mobility. Later in this discussion it will be useful to return briefly to the relationship between theoretical understanding and practical instruction—a problem that affects the reception of Clausewitz's work to the present.

In his opening lecture, the definition of the Little War is followed by a summary of war as such: Organization, weapons, methods of training, and the use of the available forces—i.e. strategy and higher tactics. This leads Clausewitz to the particular characteristics that separate the actions of small from large units. Nearly everywhere, he says, small units "maintain themselves with little effort, find it easier to hide, move more rapidly, their dispositions do not require great preparations, etc." He concludes, "Most often they have a purpose that is fairly rare for large units: observing the enemy." Despite these differences the actions of the Little War, like those of large engagements, are subject either to strategy or to tactics, two concepts that Clausewitz here defines in terms nearly identical with the words he later uses in *On War*: "Tactics we consider the use of fighting forces in combat; strategy the use to which combat is put."[8]

Subsequent lectures treat such topics as "Purpose and Organization of an Army's Outposts," "Patrols and Reconnaissance," the "Use of Entrenchments and Artillery," and other elements of the Little War, which Clausewitz regularly links with the movements and actions of large formations. Examples drawn from recent history and exercises designed by him help explain the material; some are included in the text of the lectures, but most are grouped in separate notebooks, which total 133 pages in print. The examples not only clarify, they particularize matters that might mistakenly be taken for universals. That does not prevent Clausewitz from also identifying generalities, as long as his listeners recognize that "what is called *universal* in war must always be understood to mean *most often*,"[9]—another strike against so-called laws. In the lecture "On the Character of the Little War," he notes that this kind of combat is marked by

> the strange characteristic that together with the highest degree of boldness and audacity it includes far greater aversion to danger than is common in the line ... The

single hussar or chasseur shows a degree of initiative, self-confidence, and trust in luck that a man who has always served in the line can hardly imagine ... On the other hand, he respects danger in combat more than do men in closed formations ... he draws back and seeks protection ... In large formations one must defy danger, the single individual achieves nothing with cunning and intelligence ..., by contrast, the free play of the spirit in the Little War, this adroit combination of daring and caution (I should like to say, this happy composition of audacity and fear) is what makes the Little War so particularly interesting.[10]

A remarkable statement by a Prussian officer in 1810, words that acknowledge the reality of fear and even its possible benefits, and treat the common soldier as an autonomous human being at a time when the rank and file were still subject to beatings by the drill sergeant.

Passages such as this summary of the difference between men fighting in close formations and men acting with some measure of independence show Clausewitz seeking to explain a broader conception of tactics to officers whose experience was largely if not wholly limited to service in the line—what they now heard meant for many a radical change from the accustomed. But for the process of the army's reform and renewal, his lectures had a significance that went beyond their official subject—their text carried implications for the new tactical system as a whole. Briefly, the new system had to solve the problem of how to combine individual actions of scouts and skirmishers with the mass, of achieving the collaboration of close and open formations between the line and specialists in more individual action—*Jäger*, marksmen, fusiliers, who had already, though not in large numbers, been present in the old army—but now also to enable the individual grenadier or musketeer to fight in line, in column, and at least to a limited extent to act in small groups or even individually, an ability the French Revolution had imparted, if without Prussian precision, to the new French infantry by the hundreds of thousands.

That was the system being developed by the reformers' commissions, on one of which Clausewitz served, on the new tactical doctrine, the comprehensive system that Tiedemann was teaching in his lectures. The new doctrine demanded a new kind of training. It also paralleled the shift from recruiting mercenaries and inducting the least privileged segments of the population to the conscription of citizens. Both the new manpower policies and the new tactics called for a changed treatment of the soldier, who, even as he remained the subject of an authoritarian state, was now assumed to be driven by different motives. Now not only economic necessity and administrative compulsion were to make men soldiers, but also civic duty and eventually patriotic conviction. As Clausewitz's lectures on the Little War explain its particular characteristics, special demands, and their implications for large operations of the new tactical integration, they also point to its broad social, administrative, and political consequences.

Clausewitz does not spell out these consequences, but his description of the attitudes that the Little War demands from its participants and fosters in them—enterprise, self-confidence, "the free play of the mind"—makes it clear that the soldiers whom his listeners will have to lead in future wars are no longer mechanically reacting subjects, drilled with the stick, but a new breed. In this respect, too, not only in their exposition of the tasks and methods of the Little War and in their references to the new integrated tactics, Clausewitz's lectures are a significant document of the Prussian military reforms.

In his lectures Clausewitz treats the Little War as a part of war itself, and shows that without its methods of outposts, patrols, and raids large formations can no longer function effectively when facing the increased mobility of Napoleonic tactics and operations. What his lectures do not contain is a discussion of a further kind of war, in some respects related to the Little War, but different in motives, organization, and also methods (once the limits of what is ordinarily permitted or accepted in war are crossed): revolutionary war. Clausewitz does mention revolutionary or people's war a few times—evidently the subject was not so risky that one had to hide it from French spies—but he refers to it only in passing, as a type of war that exists and is known from recent events. How then to explain Werner Hahlweg's very different interpretation in his edition of the lectures? He writes, "In respect to the country's limited resources [the Prussian patriots fully understood] that a possible successful liberation from French domination could only be achieved through a people's war or revolutionary war supported by a foreign power ... In the minds of the Prussian patriots the Little War was directly linked ... with the country's fate, it seemed the only alternative, a last resort leading to salvation. In light of these connections," Hahlweg concludes, "against this background, Clausewitz's lectures must be appraised, have their actual meaning."[11] He interprets the lectures as a disguised document of revolutionary war, or at least as preparation for such a war.

Is this interpretation justified? The reform party did indeed show an interest in popular or revolutionary war, an interest that led to organizing networks of agents and local leaders to be ready to arm the people, and to other preparatory measures for armed popular action in conjunction with regular forces. Clausewitz took part in these preparations, which two years later served as a basis for his demand of a guerrilla war in the third part of his "Declaration" or "Memorial of Confession," written shortly before he left Prussia.[12] But it seems an exaggeration of these interests and preparations to claim, in Professor Hahlweg's words, that it was the reformers' view "that a possibly successful liberation from French domination could only be achieved through a people's war or revolutionary war supported by a foreign power ... it seemed the only alternative, a last resort leading to salvation." On the contrary, it must be said that not everyone who worked for the renewal of army and state shared this opinion, and we know that in 1813 the liberation of Prussia was achieved in other ways—by regular troops and a general mobilization, in connection with Russian forces, which as they pursued the retreating French advanced beyond the Vistula into Prussia.

A tendency of military studies in the decades after 1945 may have contributed to call Hahlweg's attention to the subject of the people's war: the development of new doctrines, stimulated by the anticolonial civil wars in Vietnam and Algeria, such as that of *guerre révolutionnaire* in the French Army, and encouraged the study of irregular war in history and in the present. Today, in the early twenty-first century, similar concerns may arouse a new interest in Hahlweg's thesis that Clausewitz's lectures possessed a pronounced revolutionary character. A reading of the lectures, however, shows that this is not the case. In Clausewitz's lectures popular war is never discussed. He merely refers to the subject a few times, and then only on the margin. After 150 manuscript pages he writes under the heading "Secret Marches," "When one wants to attack, overwhelm, or reconnoiter a position or outpost, it is natural to arrange one's advance as secretly as possible." He lists the goals of these advances—bridges, magazines, the gathering of information, etc.—and concludes with the comment that "more often than used to be the case [these operations] occur in civil wars, national uprisings, etc." Fourteen pages later, under the heading "Attacks on Small Posts," he comments, "In a national uprising and defense of the kind now mounted in Spain, the kind that occurred in the Tirol, and in the civil wars in the Vendée, almost all engagements are attacks on small defensive outposts."[13] And once more, thirty-six pages later, under the heading "Capturing a General in His Quarters," he notes: "This may occur very frequently in civil wars and uprisings. Instead of rules, we shall mention only that it is not unimportant in such circumstances to target the personal safety of generals and commanders. It may create dissatisfaction and discouragement in the enemy."[14]

With these references Clausewitz shows that certain tactical actions also or often occur in people's wars. He has nothing to say about the central issues of such conflicts—how civilians are motivated to take up arms, how they are organized and trained, and how the coordination of regular troops and armed civilians is achieved—but remains in the framework of his lectures, explaining to his students the actions of the Little War, illustrated by a wealth of historical examples, and the significance of these actions for the new tactical system in general, explanations that were important as the army was reshaped at a time of imminent political and military crisis. That is not to argue that he would not have resorted to guerrilla operations in circumstances he regarded as suitable. But his lectures on the Little War contain not a single statement suggesting that Clausewitz intended the lectures as a hidden preparation for a revolutionary war, or even as a symbol of such a war. Nor is there any contemporary evidence that they were received as such.

To determine any possible deeper meaning of Clausewitz's lectures on the Little War, it is, however, not sufficient merely to analyze their content. The lectures should also be compared with other, earlier writings on the Little War. In the following review of the literature, I rely primarily on two of the earliest and best known of these works, both by officers of the French monarchy, de la Croix's *Traité de la petite guerre,* published in Paris in 1752, and Grandmaison's *La petite guerre,* which appeared in Paris four years later and was soon translated into German. Both authors discuss the Little War as an essential compound of actions in modern—that is, mid-eighteenth-century—wars, but have nothing to say about insurrections. After the Seven Years' War, Frederick the Great used Grandmaison's text in his training of General Staff officers—which suggests that the work stands at the peak of military theory of the period. A comparison of Clausewitz's lectures with the two French volumes reveals that they treat identical themes—the tactical and operational possibilities of the Little War—in language that is often remarkably similar and that conveys the same interest in practical measures, undertaken to implement the cooperation of small units with large formations. As Grandmaison writes in his introductory chapter: "That one needs light troops when facing an opponent who has them is obvious … Even more apparent is the superiority of an army with many light troops against an enemy who has none."[15]

In these and in other specifics, Clausewitz's lectures and the earlier works cover the same ground and in much the same way. In general, the volumes of de la Croix and Grandmaison, like every work on the Little War and on light troops from the second half of the eighteenth century that I have consulted, contain chapters or sections on the same topics covered in Clausewitz's lectures: the organization of small units, what officers and men must know to carry out patrols, long marches, surprise attacks, etc. The instruction the young Clausewitz received from Scharnhorst at the Institute for Military Sciences included the same matter.[16] Details may be treated differently; but on the whole the literature on the Little War is marked by a degree of unanimity that is not characteristic of the literature on strategy and operations of large units published in the same period. And neither the older works I have cited nor Clausewitz's lectures discuss revolutionary wars. The main difference between them consists in Clausewitz's wider perspective, which leads from the practices of the Little War to a recognition of war as a political-social phenomenon. The earlier works are manuals, practical introductions to a recognized area of military activity. If the leading works in the literature on the Little War are compared to the numerous articles on military subjects in Diderot's *Encyclopédie,* the first volumes of which appeared in the same years as the manuals cited above, we see that they differ in their wealth of practical experience from the average military article in the *Encyclopédie*.[17] Since they address the military reader, they are more pragmatic and less openly political.

It is a further confirmation of the nonrevolutionary character of his lectures, that Clausewitz not only does not single out the methods of the Little War as specifically revolutionary but cites or mentions favorably a number of works in the Enlightenment literature on the Little War, written by officers of the French monarchy, the United Kingdom, and of armies of the members of the Holy Roman Empire, all of whom treat the Little War as an integral part of normal interstate conflict.[18]

To be specific, both de la Croix and Grandmaison exhaustively discuss each of the three actions that Clausewitz specifically mentions as often occurring in revolutionary and people's wars. "Secret marches" are, of course, also discussed in other works on the Little War. Scharnhorst, for example, devotes a chapter of his *Military Pocketbook* to the preparation and execution of such marches, and characterizes the Little War in general with the words, "Secrecy is its main feature."[19] Such topics as methods of preparing and executing an ambush, and of capturing generals and other significant persons, the mere mention of which Hahlweg qualifies as elements of revolutionary doctrine, are treated by de la Croix, Grandmaison, and other authors as standard measures, not only of the Little War but of war in general.[20] That Grandmaison's work is dedicated to Louis XV's minister of war may be taken as merely another guarantee of its firmly monarchical character. Here it is perhaps worth noting that a tactical method or system may, but also may not, be the expression of an ideology. Tactics often give voice to a social or political reality; at other times they adjust to the most varied conditions. Does it add to our understanding of the Second World War, would it even be factually accurate, to characterize the doctrine of American infantry units as democratic, and that of the Wehrmacht as totalitarian? The history of war as well as the literature on the Little War, examples of which are cited above, demonstrate that the methods of the Little War, the natural form of a revolutionary or people's war, are an equally integral component of monarchic armies in the eighteenth and early nineteenth centuries.

Popular war was certainly a logical consequence of the ideas held by many of the more radical reformers. But the most uncompromising members of this group, even as they gave important impetus to innovation, did not always determine its course, nor did theoretical reflection always lead to the expected political and military conclusion, and Clausewitz—though in the spring of 1812 he despaired of the Prussian state, did not hesitate to express himself in extreme terms, and tried to have the king understand that the state's fighting strength was not limited to the army but rested in the entire population—was nevertheless realistic enough to show less confidence in guerrilla actions on the Prussian plains than in the reformed army, which in his lectures from 1810 until the spring of 1812 he sought to prepare for the coming war. It seems that Professor Hahlweg in his understandable interest in men's reflections on revolutionary war at the time—a subject that he has explored in a separate study—pursued their radical ideas to their logical conclusion, and made assumptions that the existing documents do not support. However Clausewitz appraised the possibilities of an uprising, his lectures do not discuss popular war. And that is not surprising. The lectures are a document of the reform movement, which called for and achieved some structural changes in state and army. That a number of reformers further speculated about launching a guerrilla war expressed a sentiment, an ideal that never reached the point of demanding the necessary far-reaching changes in government and in the political beliefs of the conservative supporters of the absolute monarchy, which in the Prussia of 1810 were not influenced by the religious considerations that played such a large, indeed decisive role in the uprisings in the Vendée.

On the other hand, considerable evidence backs Professor Hahlweg's assertion that Clausewitz's lectures contain steps towards *On War*. The sometimes very early appearance in Clausewitz's writings of ideas and concepts that over years achieve their final form in *On War*, to say nothing of formulations that are repeated nearly word for word, has long been documented—even if it is often denied or ignored in the Anglo-American literature, perhaps out of a romantic belief in the nature of sudden inspiration in the arts and sciences.[21] Hahlweg points to the presence in the lectures of such concepts as "Friction," and such formulations as the definitions of strategy and tactics. I would add that the lectures as a whole, detailed and pragmatic as they are, rest on a broad view of armed conflict, which already include features of Clausewitz's mature theory. We see this, for instance, in the comprehensive use of historical examples, which anticipate Book II, chapter 6 of *On War*, the chapter that begins with the statement "Historical examples clarify everything and also provide the best proof in the empirical sciences. This is particularly true of the art of war."[22] In *On War* Clausewitz distinguishes between examples that clarify an idea, others that show the idea in action, and historical examples that demonstrate the existence or possibility of something, or that give an account of events in the past from which lessons may be drawn. The many examples Clausewitz gives in his lectures are used for exactly these purposes. The relevant chapter in *On War* may be read as an analytic summary and discussion of the varied use of examples first employed in great numbers in his lectures on the Little War.

Beyond the functions Clausewitz ascribes to historical examples in *On War*, these references to the past express a general understanding and point of view that became the basis of his mature theories: On the one hand, war is composed of timeless elements—war as an act of force; the two types of war, limited and absolute; moral and psychological forces; major successes help bring about minor ones; etc.—but each war is dependent on the particular conditions of the time in which it is waged, and times always change, a constant change that makes timeless laws of action suspect, if not impossible. In the development of

Clausewitz's theories these references represent the function of history. They give theory broad scope, but with their specificity also draw its limits. As an example, we know that in every war, whether of a prehistoric tribe or a modern democracy, the relationship of political authority and the armed forces is a determining element; but the particular form this relationship assumes cannot be reduced to an abstraction, a single principle or rule. The timeless elements of war may be studied as abstractions; to understand them in the manifold forms they assume in reality, we must follow their course through time. In Clausewitz's theory historical examples represent the changing forms of reality that any study of war that aspires to more than superficial understanding must accommodate.

In the mass and variety of Clausewitz's work, his lectures on the Little War represent something of an exception. They are neither theory—although based on the beginnings of a comprehensive theoretical view of war—nor military history—although historical examples deepen and strengthen the analysis of the little war. They have an immediate didactic purpose. But their place in the history of military ideas rests not solely in their content. The sources Clausewitz used also deserve attention, and it is worth noting that in his lectures Clausewitz drew extensively on the literature of an earlier age—as historical examples, but also as examples of actions to be performed now or in the near future.

If we consider his lectures in the General War School from this perspective, we can see that they illustrate elements in the development of his ideas on what war is and how war can be studied realistically and at the same time systematically. By his early twenties, as he reflected on his first campaigns, and as he moved from reading historical works to writing his own first historical studies, Clausewitz came to realize that some elements of war did not vary from generation to generation, while in other respects the conduct of war responded to, and was linked with, the passage of time. Innovations in weapons and equipment could affect methods of fighting, but the effect of social, political, and cultural changes could be as great or greater. Between 1789 and 1800 no new weapon, no improvement in equipment or advances in their method of manufacture had a major impact on the conduct of war, which nevertheless was adjusting to exploit the new possibilities and cope with the new dangers that resulted from the rise of novel and newly intense ideologies, of political events and social developments. For an understanding of war as such it was essential to recognize both the permanent elements of conflict and their subjection and adaptation to the reality of constant change. In his lectures on the nature and practice of the Little War, Clausewitz used the literature of an earlier age repeatedly, and not merely as a source, but in reference to the practical needs of the present. He was able to do this because in Europe after the ideological crises of the Counter-Reformation and before the social and political upheaval of the French Revolution, significant change still required a long passage of time. In Central Europe, the countryside, the roads, weapons, the social position and attitudes of the rural population remained throughout the eighteenth century and some years beyond pretty much as they had been earlier, so that in 1810 it was still possible to analyze and explain the tactics of the Little War and the duties of outposts and patrols with the help of writings of the Seven Years' War. Traditional conditions and attitudes were not yet outdated. If we consider the lectures from this point of view, they appear both as the realistic, pragmatic complement of Clausewitz's theoretical considerations, and as emblematic of his refined understanding of history as well as of the relevance of this understanding for his thinking on war in general. His lectures on the Little War with their extensive analysis and application of old ideas and methods to current and future action become an example of Clausewitz's undogmatic mind, which has recognized constant change and simultaneous permanence of war in history, and now moves forward within their twofold reality.

Notes

1. *Das Preussische Heer der Befreiungskriege*, I, *Das Preussische Heer im Jahr 1812*, ed. Grosser Generalstab, Kriegsgeschichtliche Abteilung II, Berlin, 1912, 50.
2. Carl von Clausewitz to August N. von Gneisenau, 24 June 1810, in Carl von Clausewitz, *Schriften–Aufsätze–Studien–Briefe,* Göttingen, 1966–1990, I, 628.
3. Carl von Clausewitz "Meine Vorlesungen über den kleinen Krieg…," ibid., 208–599.
4. Ibid., 226–456.
5. Ibid., 228, 230.
6. Ibid., 231–33.
7. Carl von Clausewitz, *On War*, trans. and ed. by Michael Howard and Peter Paret, Princeton, 1976, Book I, ch. 1, 86.
8. Clausewitz, "Vorlesungen," *Schriften*, I, 235. "Tactics teaches the use of armed forces in the engagement, strategy the use of engagements for the object of the war," *On War*, Book II, ch.1, 128.
9. "In der Kriegskunst … sind es immer die *meisten Fälle* welche für das *allgemeine* [Clausewitz's emphasis] genommen werden müssen." "Vorlesungen," *Schriften*, I, 234.
10. Ibid., 238–39. Seven years earlier, in his answer to a test, the young Clausewitz referred to the fear experienced by soldiers as a reality not simply to be repressed but to be understood; see the second essay in this volume.
11. Werner Hahlweg, Introduction, in Clausewitz, "Vorlesungen," *Schriften*, I, 210.
12. See the second essay in this volume. The first two parts of the document are published in Carl von Clausewitz, *Historical and Political Writings*, trans. and ed. Peter Paret and Daniel Moran, Princeton, 1992, 285–303.
13. Clausewitz, "Vorlesungen," *Schriften*, I, 394. Hahlweg interprets these sentences as follows: "In his lectures on the Little War, Clausewitz alerts his listeners in the Berlin War Academy to the educational utilization of the Spanish war [ibid., I, 601n8], which seems to place far too much weight on Clausewitz's brief observation."
14. Clausewitz, "Vorlesungen," *Schriften*, I, 440.
15. M. de Grandmaison, *La petite guerre ou traité du service des troupes légères en campagne,* Paris, 1756, 6, 8.

16. See the second essay in the present work.
17. Apart from the great survey *"Guerre"* of Lieutenant General Marquis de Tressac in the seventh volume (1757), who appraises the Little War in the following words: "Nothing contributes more to an army's security than small, independently acting units" (993), the *Encyclopédie* contains approximately 150 articles on military matters, among them an article *"Petite Guerre* (1765, vol. XII, 466) from an anonymous contributor, who again emphasizes the "absolute necessity" of the Little War to maintain an army's security.
18. Among the publications Clausewitz frequently mentions in the lectures are Andrew Emmerich, *The Partisan in War,* London, 1789, on 292, 316, 355, 382, etc., and Johann von Ewald, *Abhandlung von dem Dienst der leichten Truppen,* Leipzig, 1790, on 282, 295, 299, 351, 384, etc. An earlier version, *Abhandlung über den kleinen Krieg,* was published in Kassel in 1785.
19. Gerhard Johann David Scharnhorst, *Militairisches Taschenbuch zum Gebrauch im Felde,* Hanover, 1792, 53, 39–45. In his final lecture Clausewitz mentions Scharnhorst's *Pocketbook* first among the works "that to greater or lesser extent are distinguished by originality ... No other work contains such a wealth of historical examples one can say it contains not a single unnecessary word." *Schriften,* I, 445–49.
20. Grandmaison, *La petite guerre,* 57–60, 169, 182, 186, 211, 307, etc.
21. Examples are the archival discoveries and analyses by Hans Rothfels in 1922 and Eberhard Kessel in 1937.
22. Clausewitz, *On War,* Book II, ch. 6, 170.

6

Two Historians on Defeat in War and Its Causes

Two historians, one 134 years before the other, serve in wars in which their armies are defeated, and the states for which they fight collapse. They begin immediately to write accounts of the campaigns that have just ended in disaster. That both fought in previous wars and in their writings addressed major historical issues gives them the tools they need. The similarities in their conditions and reactions are remarkable, as are the differences. The earlier historian is twenty-six years old when the war soon to be his subject breaks out in 1806. The other is fifty-three when his country is overrun in 1940. The younger man's analytic gifts are already evident in his first essays; the older has long been an original and influential historian. As they start to record the recent past, the younger man allows himself few emotional responses to the events he describes; the older gives a fuller, more personal account. He begins and ends his manuscript between June and September 1940, shortly after the surrender of the armed forces in which he served; but his book does not appear until after his death. The younger historian is captured, writes a compressed study of the campaign within two months of its major battles, and sends it to a journal, which publishes it in three installments. After being released, his duties and other literary work prevent him from returning to the subject for seventeen years, at which time he intends to write a comprehensive history of the political events that lead to the war, the war itself, and its immediate aftermath, then changes his mind and limits his manuscript to the campaign of 1806, which is largely based on his previous study. Because he is highly critical of the men in charge, his manuscript is not published until fifty-six years after his death. The other historian, demobilized in July 1940, joins the resistance, is eventually taken prisoner, and then tortured and shot by the descendants of the soldiers with whom the first historian served six generations earlier.

By birth, both authors belonged to privileged segments of society, yet each faced social handicaps. In accord with family tradition, the earlier historian,

Carl von Clausewitz, claimed noble descent.[1] His father, son of a professor of theology at the University of Halle, served as lieutenant in a Prussian infantry regiment during the Seven Years' War. After demobilization he was retired for being unable to document his title of nobility, and transferred to the customs and excise administration. The family's ambiguous situation was resolved by two events: the early death of the former lieutenant's father and the remarriage of his mother. Her second husband, a Prussian colonel, came from a well-known noble family. His influence could not salvage the lieutenant's military career, but enabled three of his four sons, among them Carl von Clausewitz, to enter the army as officer cadets. The Clausewitz family's noble status was at last officially accepted in 1827, not on the basis of documentation, but in acknowledgment of the brothers' successful military careers. Two became generals; the third, a colonel, received the courtesy rank of major-general on retirement. At the time, the change from undocumented assumption of a title to its recognition occurred more than once in the Prussian service elite, which expanded in step with the expansion of the state. In Clausewitz's generation middle-class officers were promoted to the most senior positions in the army, and ennobled in the process.

The other historian, Marc Bloch, descended on both sides of his family from Alsatian Jews.[2] In 1793 a paternal ancestor founded the family's tradition of patriotic French citizenship by fighting in the forces that defended the French occupation of Mainz against a Prussian army in which Clausewitz served as a newly promoted ensign. Bloch's father, who left Alsace after the Franco-Prussian War to avoid becoming a German subject, taught Greek and Roman antiquities at the University of Lyon, and rose to be a professor of ancient history at the École Normale Supérieure in Paris. Marc Bloch's encounter with French anti-Semitism and Carl von Clausewitz's awareness of his family's dubious hold on privilege seem above all to have sharpened the two men's observations on their societies, which ranged from skeptical analysis to outright condemnation—harsh judgments in which the recognition of human weakness is sharpened by personal disappointment and disillusion.

In their two works Clausewitz and Bloch repeatedly introduce social and psychological observations with references to themselves and their backgrounds. The authors' engagement drives their interpretations forward and gives them their peculiar edgy knowledge. Early in his work Bloch turns to his family and childhood to explain his perception of an element that is—or should have been—central to the events he recounts: "I was brought up in the tradition of patriotism, which found no more fervent champions than the Jews of the Alsatian exodus [after the Franco-Prussian War in which Germany acquired Alsace Lorraine]."[3] Clausewitz interrupts his critique of the Prussian Army's formalism, which he holds in part responsible for its defeat in 1806, by defending himself against possible accusations of prejudice with the assurance that: "From the beginning, *national* feeling and even *caste* sentiment [author's emphases] were as pronounced and firmly rooted in the author as the lessons of life can make them. Further, the author must say that he always fared better in the Prussian army than he deserved ... and if he soon came to think differently about Prussia's military institutions than most of his comrades, this was simply the result of reflection."[4] The two men would not deny that defeat affected their feelings, even as they assured readers and critics that what may seem to be emotional exaggerations are the outcome of deeply felt but rationally considered experience.

More firmly than these explanations, the analytic foundations of their books indicate that Clausewitz and Bloch would not allow emotion to guide their interpretations. They are too focused on understanding. Yet at times—more often with Bloch—the depth and explosiveness of their feelings break through the language. We could think that this is already suggested by the titles of their books, had Bloch himself named his work *L'étrange défaite*. But the title, *Strange Defeat*, was selected by others after his death, and reflects their sense that the defeat was "strange," odd, not to be expected, which is the opposite of the book's message. Clausewitz's title, on the other hand, *Nachrichten über Preussen in seiner grossen Katastrophe*, usually translated as *Observations on Prussia in Her Great Catastrophe*, is his own. It breaks with the formality of the time in which the work was written, by naming its subject not a lost campaign but a political disaster. Feelings—here outrage, disappointment, a sense of betrayal—often energize scholarly interpretations, even as they offer critics a target. Less common is the collaboration of frankly expressed emotions with firm analysis, a double characteristic that makes the two books scholarly works yet also open personal statements.

...

Clausewitz in 1806 and Bloch in 1940 were about equal in rank—one a staff captain, the junior level of that rank in the Prussian Army, the other a captain. Not only their previous experience of war, but also their current duties gave them a measure of understanding the events in which they found themselves beyond that of most company-grade officers. After some temporary assignments, Bloch was transferred to First Army Headquarters near the British segment of the front, attached to the section in charge of transport, labor, and supply, duties that kept him informed and enabled him to deduce larger operational decisions and even strategic considerations. His function, he noted, called for "intelligence and diplomacy."[5] Clausewitz held what might appear to be a modest position as adjutant of the commander of a grenadier battalion; but the commander was a royal prince, and access to senior officers and army headquarters flowed naturally from his status.

In tone and content the three articles Clausewitz published on the campaign of 1806 cast light on his future book-length treatment of the subject. The matter-of-fact title of the articles, *Historische Briefe über die grossen Kriegsereignisse im Oktober 1806* [*Historical Letters on the Major Military Events in October 1806*] reflects Clausewitz's sober analysis of a campaign largely lost before it began.[6] With Austria's defeat in 1805, Prussia remained Napoleon's last potential opponent in Central Europe, and inevitably became his next victim. After the Austerlitz campaign, units of the Grande Armée stayed deep in Germany, and in 1806 were able to advance on Prussia from the south. The Prussian Army, numerically weaker than the French and too slow to respond effectively, withdrew north towards Berlin, and on 14 October its separate parts were defeated in simultaneous battles at Jena and Auerstedt, which ended with the retreating forces colliding, a temporary breakdown of control, and the occupation of Berlin. Despite these disasters and the occupation of much of the country, the war continued until the following summer, eight months that Clausewitz's study did not cover. The articles, with their evenhanded treatment of both sides, form the basis of the more extensive treatment in his later book, now embedded in a very critical and outspoken analysis of Prussia's political and military leadership and of the state's institutions and social structures.

After disclaiming absolute accuracy for his *Historical Letters* and welcoming corrections, Clausewitz states his major theme: although the public finds the Prussian defeats "shocking and incredible," they are not difficult to explain.[7] Numerical and strategic inferiority might have been balanced by greater mobility and exceptional leadership, but neither was present. Shock and psychological exhaustion turned the twin defeat into a rout. Clausewitz draws his conclusions about the weaker army's institutional flaws in temperate terms; his comments on Prussian operational decisions are also relatively mild.[8] He ends by returning to his original premise: considering the nature of the opposing forces and the disparity in strengths, the Prussian defeat was not surprising. On the contrary, it should have been expected. His account tries to show "that the *astonishing result* came about in a *natural way*." The mistakes that occurred could be corrected in the future, and he appeals to his German readers to collect themselves "and *not despair of your fate* [author's emphases]."[9]

The *Historical Letters* are not the strongest of Clausewitz's early writings. Narrative and analysis are not always smoothly combined; his opening assurance that he seeks objectivity is too long, as he himself notes. But his account of the campaign has never been seriously challenged: since the Prussian Army, with its operational and tactical limitations, faced a stronger, more mobile opponent advancing from a position of strategic superiority, even hard fighting could not prevent defeat. To find this strange was to be blinded by the reputation the army had gained under Frederick the Great.

In his later book on the campaign Clausewitz further develops these points, and now also looks for the causes of the army's limitations, which he locates ultimately in Prussian society, politics, and leadership. Beginning with the book's title and its opening paragraph, his *Observations on Prussia* is military history as total history. The book of 121 pages, not counting the introduction by the unnamed editor, an officer of the German general staff, is divided into four chapters. The final chapter, a little over half of the total text, gives a thoughtful account of the campaign of 1806, confirmed in its essentials and most of its details generations later by French and German general-staff studies of the campaign.[10] But to a considerable degree the war was shaped by the matter of the preceding chapters: "A Glance at the Spirit of the Army and the Administration," "Characterizations of the Leading Personalities," and "Background of and Preparations for the War."

In the first chapter Clausewitz examines the Prussian Army and government, and finds both wanting. "All unprejudiced observers of Prussia concluded ... that the state was wrecked by its institutions. A vain, immoderate faith in these institutions made it possible to overlook that their vitality was gone. The machine could still be heard clattering along ... [yet] no one asked if it was still doing its job."[11] The passage is a good example of Clausewitz's mature style: direct, alert to cause and effect, moving easily from declarative statements to figures of speech, from the plain to the elevated, from stating a fact to its ironic evaluation. A critical examination of Prussia's government follows: absolutism with overlapping ministries and agencies, none in full control of the matters it administers, the king ruling by decree without responsible advisors. Clausewitz dismisses attempts to limit the power of the nobility and bring competent members of the middle class into government as "superficial gilding," and concludes that poor government and poor administration create a poor army: "More than any other institution [the army] had succumbed to the lassitude of tradition and detail."[12] A long list of the army's flaws begins with the system of forced recruitment and the high rate of desertion associated with it, as well as its many exemptions, which, as Clausewitz had noted earlier, invites corruption and social injustice. From there he moves to the practice of foreign recruitment and the long period of service, leading to overage officers and men, and then aims with hyperbolic accuracy at a condition that is always his preferred target, the tyranny of form over substance: "The soldier's weapon was kept scrupulously clean, barrels were painstakingly polished ... stocks varnished every year; but the muskets were the worst in Europe.... Everything was tied up in endless red tape ... the insistent observance of external forms caused people to lose sight of what really mattered."[13] Finally he turns to society, the character of which, he writes, the state should not have ignored at a time "when the support of all classes of the population was essential."[14] He doubts that far-reaching reforms could have been introduced as war was about to begin, but both government and army would have gained if the king had at least appointed new, capable, and energetic ministers—an oddly moderate conclusion to the thunderclaps of his analysis, perhaps explained by the fact that he was writing at a time of conservative reaction when he himself was accused of dangerous radicalism.

The second chapter with its portraits of the leading figures in government and the army became famous decades before the book was published. Historians with access to the manuscript quoted or used for background these miniature analyses, some several pages in length, others no more than a few sentences, in which Clausewitz characterizes certain individuals, most of whom he had come to know in the last years before the war, when his duties brought him in touch with senior officers and officials. A few who continued to play a role after 1806 he encountered again as friends or antagonists during the last campaigns against Napoleon or later, when he served as director of the War Academy in Berlin.

Excerpts from two of the shorter portraits suggest how Clausewitz used biography to define the politically dominant society of these years. First his description of General Rüchel, his first regimental commander, a corps commander at Jena whose traditionalism contributed to the defeat: "Frederick the Great was his every third word. The spirit of the old king raised to dominance after the Seven Years' War and personally infused into the army in Potsdam—a certain sternness and precision, which occasionally picks on an insignificant detail to show that nothing is overlooked, a certain thunder-and-lightning military rhetoric—all this was exaggerated in Rüchel.... [H]e was convinced that with courage and determination Prussian troops employing Frederician tactics could overrun everything that had emerged from the unsoldierly French Revolution.... General Rüchel might have been termed a concentrated acid of pure Prussianism."[15]

Another portrait, this one of Count Haugwitz, dismisses a figure who stood for years at the center of the state's foreign policy in two sentences: "A short man in his forties, with pleasant features and agreeable manners that expressed superficiality, irresponsibility, falseness; but these blended so perfectly with the man's calm, gentlemanly behavior that there was nothing comic about him. Such was Count Haugwitz's demeanor; and that was also his personality."[16]

Men of this kind, without exceptional abilities to make up for their common flaws, could hardly contend with French diplomatic and military power, as harnessed and driven forward by Napoleon. In the third chapter of the *Observations on Prussia*, Clausewitz traces the inconsistency in Prussian foreign policy from the Peace of Basle in 1795 to the outbreak of war in 1806. By maintaining the neutrality of northern Germany while not supporting Austria, Prussia isolated itself as French power spread across Europe, eventually to face Napoleon alone, but for the forced support of Saxony, which did not last beyond the opening battles—a political disaster that "was due entirely to [Prussia's] own policies."[17] His analysis then shifts to Prussian society: "The mass of the people, the workers and peasants, were still not truly aware of what was going on." But among

> the upper ... [or] educated classes' interest in politics had grown more intense, so that by the end of 1805 three parties emerged. The first admired French institutions, French glory and brilliance, and would have considered it a good thing for Europe to be placed under the tutelage of France. *Thus, no war with France!* The second party had the same objective, but only because it dreaded nothing so much as seeing the prevailing peace and tranquility disturbed, and ... feared to risk the strength of the Prussian state on a dangerous and unpromising course of action. *Thus again, no war with France!* The third party saw French progress in Europe as leading toward a universal monarchy that threatened Prussia's existence. Therefore, *war with France!*[18]

In the end, Prussia, her society and government divided, stumbled into a war for which politically, diplomatically, and militarily the state was unprepared. It was this level of criticism and its uncompromising conclusion that made publication of the book impossible during its author's life and for decades afterwards.

• • •

Locating the causes of defeat in military inadequacy, but ultimately in weaknesses in government and society is also a message of Marc Bloch's *Strange Defeat*. He finds a basic military flaw in the tendency of senior French officers to fight the Second World War with expectations formed by lessons learned in the First. But Bloch himself was marked professionally and personally by experiences gained between 1914 and 1918. In a famous article he termed war "the historian's great laboratory," particularly of collective attitudes and behavior; and in its account of his service in 1939 and 1940 *L'étrange défaite* continues the *Souvenirs de guerre, 1914–1915,* the first part of which he wrote in 1915.[19] Now, rather than write another volume of personal reminiscences or a comprehensive military history of the war, he searches for reasons the French fought as they did, based on what he witnessed as a soldier in the new war and on his knowledge as a citizen and historian. His book, somewhat longer than Clausewitz's *Observations on Prussia,* is divided into three chapters, arranged to suggest the record of a judicial hearing or trial. In the first chapter the author identifies himself and briefly traces his background, his professional life, and his military service. The second long chapter, over half of the whole, entitled "One of the Vanquished Gives Evidence," is a wide-ranging account of his experiences in 1939 and 1940, leading to comments and conclusions on the French conduct of the war, from administrative and tactical details to the largest issues of strategy and policy. In the last chapter, "A Frenchman Examines His Conscience," Bloch analyzes the country's political and intellectual elites, and holds them—and with them himself—responsible for the country's flaws that led to defeat. In the end, witness, accused, and judge become one.[20]

Although Bloch's book is clearly structured, the text of the first two chapters is somewhat diffused. In its tone and its readiness to move back and forth between topics, interrupting one train of thought to pursue another, it differs from Clausewitz's consecutive and restrained narrative. The language is informal, voluble, at times full of pathos; Gerard Hopkins's too literal English translation does not obscure its largely conversational character but retains little of Bloch's elegant precision. Parts read like an early draft, which perhaps they were, and the tension and danger under which they were written seem palpable. In the first chapter Bloch identifies himself as a professional historian, a Jew, whose great-grandfather and father fought for France, as he did in the First World War, and as a patriot whose "deepest emotions are inextricably bound up" with his country—an introduction that sums up his intellectual and emotional position, both now threatened by defeat and anti-Semitism. He outlines his various military assignments in 1939 and 1940, his combat experiences, his evacuation from Dunkirk and return to Normandy, where, changing into civilian clothes, he stays in Rennes as German units occupy the town, before he makes his way back to his family.

Bloch opens the second chapter by stating the general theme of his work and its resolution: "We have just suffered such a defeat as no one would have believed possible.... Whatever the deep-seated causes of the disaster ... the immediate cause (as I shall attempt to explain later) was the utter incompetence of the High Command."[21] He identifies conditions and incidents, down to such details as words heard or gestures observed, that point to the nature and causes of the disaster. Criticisms of French strategy and operations alternate with accounts of incidents he witnessed that provided him with clues to the attitudes that dominated the senior commanders and their staffs: "Our leaders ... were incapable of thinking in terms of a *new* war.... The ruling idea of the Germans in the conduct of this war was speed. We, on the other hand, did our thinking in terms of yesterday or the day before," which sounds like nothing so much as Clausewitz's complaints in 1806.[22] Descriptions of German tank tactics are joined to critical comments on French military education, the good and bad aspects of the "paper routine of our military staffs," the generally insufficient reactions to German initiatives, and numerous observations on the discipline, routine, and realism or lack of it in the conduct of regimental, division, and army headquarters, which Bloch either tried to correct or helplessly witnessed as the German offensive advanced. Interspersed are discussions of the fighting itself, such as Bloch's appraisal of the relative effectiveness of artillery or machine gun fire, or bombing, in which he again draws on a specific experience to illustrate a larger issue:

> I underwent my baptism of fire in 1940 ... on 22 May on a road in Flanders.... On the morning of the day in question, the convoy of which my car formed part was first machine-gunned from the air and then bombed. The machine-gunning, though it killed a man quite close to me, left me more or less unmoved ... [still] I was a good deal relieved when the storm of bullets passed. But all through that particular episode my uneasiness had been much more a matter of intellect than of instinct.... The bombing attack, so far as I am aware, killed no one ... Nevertheless it left me profoundly shaken.

From these particulars he deduces that the Germans did not primarily use aerial bombardment to kill, but rather to terrify, which in turn contributed to the effect of their offensive. Unlike Hitler, he concludes, the French high command was not interested in gauging and acting on their enemy's psychology.[23]

If Bloch does not offer his readers a comprehensive account of German and French strategy and operations in "this bungled and tragic war," what he does give them may be as valuable: a vivid impression of the inability of French military institutions and culture to counter the threat they faced—the more dangerous because so much of it consisted of the unfamiliar.[24] There have been many personal accounts of the campaign of 1940; but Bloch's recollections reach a different level of reality, as the historian lying in a ditch showered with dirt by an exploding shell, uncomfortable and anxious, tries to analyze the military, political, and cultural causes of his experience and their implications for his country. The confusion and failures, the energies of entire armies wasted in inadequate preparation and action, the muddle that was French resistance in May and June 1940, come to life in the physicality, intelligence, and the degree of disorder marking Bloch's account.

In contrast, his final chapter, much shorter than the second, is a well-organized essay. The chapter's seemingly simple opening sentence, "In no nation is any professional group ever entirely responsible for its own actions," expands Bloch's previous rejection of the senior military leadership into criticism of something far larger. To identify the basic reasons for the defeat he feels he must look beyond the high command and the various staffs, to French society as such. The military chiefs "could be only what the totality of the social *fact*, as it existed in France, permitted them to be."[25] He complains that "something had been lost of that fervent fraternity in danger that meant so much to most of us in the old 1914 days."[26] He singles out the inadequacy of various segments of French society: the country's leaders, "individually and as a class," lacked the necessary determination—the "ruthless heroism"—the times demanded, an example being the failure to call up and train sufficient forces before 1940. The trade unions "thought first and foremost about selling their labor at the highest price"; they, like big business, were infected by the narrow self-interest of the petite bourgeoisie.[27] The list is interrupted by one of Bloch's many observations that move from specific detail to universal recognition and make the previous chapter as interesting as it is cluttered: in June he sees "hordes of wretched men wandering about the streets in an effort to get back to their homes. All of them were carrying loads far heavier than they could cope with."[28] The reason, he explains, is that the left-luggage offices in the railway stations were closed so as not to impose overtime or heavier work than usual on their staffs. To the historian, men in the street, burdened with suitcases, reveal the egotism that has poisoned a nation's society! He deplores the unrealistic nature of pacifism, scorns the contradictions of French communism, and grieves over the ignorance of the public, for which he blames newspapers, the bourgeoisie's traditional effort to keep the masses ignorant, as well as inadequate education and flawed scholarship. The political system of the Third Republic ("It was entirely owing to our ministers and our assemblies that we were ... ill prepared for war.") also shaped the social and political power of the *grandes écoles*, one further aspect of a fragmented society. The bourgeoisie shut itself off from the common people, whose views were not heard by their political leaders, for which, in a return to earlier criticism, he holds teachers, including himself, largely responsible.[29] He concludes the chapter with a declaration of confidence in the future, based on the forces that inspired and accompanied him throughout his book: his belief in French civilization and history. Having already cited Condorcet on the need for an educated public to be free to discuss even the most fundamental constitutional issues, he now calls on the teachings of Montesquieu and the French Revolution: "A state founded on the people needs a mainspring, and that mainspring is virtue."[30] He believes in the reality of collective goodness, and appeals to it—an appeal as daring to make and as difficult to respond to positively in the twentieth century as it was in the eighteenth.

• • •

In their studies of defeat and its causes, Bloch and Clausewitz begin from contrasting starting points and follow separate routes to reach similar conclusions. Bloch, a scholar whose work was already leaving a profound imprint on his discipline, possessed the psychic freedom and intellectual independence to respond in his latest and last book to challenging events that differed in essence from the subjects he had addressed until then. For Clausewitz history was another and essential dimension of reality, but also auxiliary to his central intellectual concerns, and despite his ability to strike out on paths that departed from contemporary practice, his work left no immediate impact on the discipline. His most significant achievement as historian may have been the recognition of the importance of an even-handed view of the past, a view that powered his approach to the theoretical analysis of war. In *Strange Defeat* Bloch above all addresses French society at war and the social dimensions of the French armed services; his discussions of strategy and operations are fragmentary and incomplete. In *Observations on Prussia* Clausewitz expands his early study of the campaign into a comprehensive analytic narrative, preceded by chapters on the elements that shaped the actions of the Prussian state and army, their leaders, and the political aims they pursued. In explaining the defeats, neither writer ignores the relative strengths of the opponents or the consequence of unforeseen events, and both recognize other causes in society and its political institutions, of which the military and their actions are an extension.

How the two authors identify and interpret these causes reflects not only their personalities, but the nature of the subjects they study and the times in which they write. Bloch's interpretations are more detailed, thicker than Clausewitz's, in part because the society and politics of a parliamentary republic in the industrial age may impose somewhat different demands on the historian than do those of a preindustrial absolute monarchy. Clausewitz's exemplary and clear biographical miniatures may be taken as analytic equivalents of Bloch's more layered explorations of the various interest groups in French society. *Strange Defeat* in its discontinuities and pathos, its lack of distance between subject and presentation, is very modern. The detachment, leavened with irony, of Clausewitz's *Observations on Prussia,* whatever his particular topic and its practical and emotional impact, springs from the intellectual culture of an earlier age.

From the start, the interactions of social and political factors with war in 1806 and 1940 were obvious to Clausewitz and Bloch, as they would be to anyone—which is not to say that such interactions do not pose problems to the historian. History as a discipline demands a measure of specialization. To concentrate is to be realistic, even if that realism can be inhibiting, as at times it was for Bloch. Early on in his teaching and writing he became dissatisfied with the practice of dividing history into compartments, and as he borrowed ideas and methods from other disciplines, he also expanded the limits and thus the significance of the particular subject. A century earlier Clausewitz, even in his first studies of campaigns and war, included nonmilitary explanations of military events—a step more easily taken before than after the professionalization of history in the nineteenth century. The idea that war cannot be understood as an isolated element in human affairs became a constant in Clausewitz's many histories, as it is basic to his theories. In his interpretations of the character and use of armed force, he pays attention as a matter of course not only to the personalities of the leading figures, and to diplomacy and politics, but also to society and culture. If in *Observations on Prussia* he devotes more space than he does elsewhere to institutions, society, and politics, relative to the account and interpretation of the campaign, his method of analyzing them and their relations to the armed forces and their actions is that of his work in its entirety. *Strange Defeat*, on the other hand, is more of an exception in Bloch's oeuvre. It has even been suggested that the work repudiates his earlier writings, which did not pay much attention to the "human and individual elements" so prominent in *Strange Defeat*.[31] A difference certainly exists, but in part it may derive from Bloch's subject, the crisis of 1940, which is unlike the long social and cultural developments he explored in his medieval histories. And even when he addresses the collapse of the Republic, his analyses of collective attitudes and reactions as a means of identifying and interpreting specific issues and events appear to be in accord with his earlier work.

However often their interpretations have been discussed and tested, Bloch's *Strange Defeat* and Clausewitz's *Observations on Prussia* are now part of the historical record. In their two books the authors confront the intellectually and emotionally complex issue of severe military defeat of their own society, defeats they personally experienced. Both locate the source of the military collapse not only in the actions of the armed forces, but also in the nature and behavior of their societies at war, societies that to an extent they represent, and that at the same time they observe and judge. Intellectually and emotionally they are aware of the infinity of links between society and its armed force, know that one cannot be understood without the other, and seek to do justice to both. Their works are history in the round. Despite the many differences in the two military defeats they analyze, they also agree in their recognition and interpretation of such major disasters as opportunities for the defeated side to recast itself, correct weaknesses, and advance to new strengths. Of course, that recognition coincides with their wishes. Each writer is driven not only by the need to explain the defeats to himself and to his eventual readers; he also wants to change their consequences—Bloch by assisting in the recovery of French independence and by upholding the ideal of a more just society, Clausewitz by explaining the need for political and military reform, which will lead not only to Prussia's restoration but eventually may bring about a more cohesive and autonomous Germany. They analyze the past so as to recover from it. Despite the honesty with which they pursue their goal of understanding, that remains a dangerous combination of motives. Even as partisanship energizes their work, it may conflict with objectivity.

Each author resolves this problem in his own way. Clausewitz emphasizes military organization and function, and although these reflect social conditions and attitudes, their specificity allows him to stay within boundaries marked by the issue of effectiveness: what works and what doesn't—however much it may be valued by this or that interest group. Bloch is inspired and burdened by the grandiose but hard to define and harder to realize concepts of social fraternity and political responsibility. His violent death—not killed in combat but murdered—denied him the opportunity to move beyond the writing of *Strange Defeat* and take part as a scholar and as a citizen in further efforts to express and realize his beliefs. Clausewitz's early study, written immediately after the lost campaign, and his later, much expanded history of the same events and their causes, bracket his engagement with history over the years, an example of the place that interpreting the past had in his intellectual life.

Clausewitz's and Bloch's books are powerful histories of the defeats that are their subjects, as well as powerful expressions of the times in which they were written. *Strange Defeat* gives voice to the collapse of the Third French Republic; *Observations on Prussia* announces an early stage of German political cohesion, as the French Revolution, Napoleon, and the opposition they arouse reshape the political structure of Central Europe. The two books are driven by sudden crises, caused and accompanied by long-term trends. They reveal both authors as one in their recognition of the power of broad perspectives in history. They also show each in his individuality as a historian, and more than that as a representative of strong currents in European history that extend far beyond the scholarly occupation with the past. In Clausewitz we witness the energies of persistent, constantly replenishing elites; in Bloch the long course of still incomplete Jewish assimilation. As historians who themselves are part of their studies, the two men link *Strange Defeat* and *Observations on Prussia* to their individual lives and to the broad stream of history.

Notes

1. On the complex history of the Clausewitz family, see the third revised edition of my *Clausewitz and the State,* Princeton, 2007, xi–xii, 17–17.
2. On Marc Bloch's antecedents, see Carol Fink, *Marc Bloch: A Life in History,* Cambridge, 1989, 1–12.
3. Marc Bloch, *Strange Defeat,* trans. Gerard Hopkins, Oxford, 1949, 3.
4. Carl von Clausewitz, *Nachrichten über Preussen in seiner grossen Katastrophe,* Kriegsgeschichtliche Einzelschriften, X, Berlin, 1888. An English translation of the first three chapters "Observations on Prussia in Her Great Catastrophe" is included in Carl von Clausewitz, *Historical and Political Writings,* trans. and ed. Peter Paret and Daniel Moran, Princeton, 1992. Quotations are from this edition; the quoted passage is on 40.
5. Bloch, *Strange Defeat,* 8.
6. Carl von Clausewitz, *Historische Briefe über die grossen Kriegsereignisse im Oktober 1806,* ed. Joachim Niemeyer, Bonn, 1977.
7. Ibid., 32.
8. Ibid., 65–66.
9. Ibid., 71, 73.
10. For comparisons of Clausewitz's figures of the opposing strengths with those of later historians, see my *Clausewitz and the State,* 344–45, n27.
11. Clausewitz, *Historical and Political Writings,* 32.

12. Ibid., 36.
13. Ibid., 37, 39.
14. Ibid., 41–42.
15. Ibid., 45–66. As a small example of the complex coexistence of tradition and modernity in 1806, it may be noted that the same Rüchel whose views on war were defined by the manual was also an advocate of improvements in the army's military schools, not only for officer but also for the rank and file.
16. Ibid., 58.
17. Ibid., 73.
18. Ibid., 74.
19. Marc Bloch, "Réflexions d'un historien sur les fausses nouvelles de la guerre," in Marc Bloch, *Mélanges historiques,* Paris, 1963, I, 45.
20. On page 61 of his excellent monograph on Bloch in his cultural and historical context, *Ein Historiker im 20. Jahrhundert: Marc Bloch* (Frankfurt, 1995), Ulrich Raulff suggests an Enlightenment model for the identity of judge and accused: that of Rousseau judging himself. Raulff has also edited the German edition of *Strange Defeat, Die seltsame Niederlage* (Frankfurt, 1992), with an important introduction that traces some of the work's intellectual forerunners. In it he suggests that *Strange Defeat* breathes a similarly combative spirit as the otherwise rather different memoranda Clausewitz wrote in the spring of 1812, in which he explained that he was leaving the Prussian service to avoid having to fight for rather than against Napoleon, and appealed to the Prussian king to change his policies. On the memoranda, see my *Clausewitz and the State,* 215–19.
21. Bloch, *Strange Defeat,* 25.
22. Ibid., 37.
23. Ibid., 54–58; the quoted passage is from 55.
24. Ibid., 8.
25. Ibid., 126.
26. Ibid., 132.
27. Ibid., 134–35.
28. Ibid., 139.
29. Ibid., 169.
30. Ibid., 152, 176.
31. Bryce Lyon, "Marc Bloch: Did He Repudiate *Annales* History?" *Journal of Medieval History* 11 (1985): 190.

Bibliography

Anonymous, "Clausewitz, Carl von," *Real-Encyclopädie oder Conversations-Lexicon*, 5th edition, I, Leipzig, 1822.
Anonymous, "Clausewitz, Carl von," *Real-Encyclopädie oder Conversation-Lexicon*, 6th edition, I, Leipzig, 1827.
Anonymous, "General-Lieutenant Rühle von Lilienstern," *Militair-Wochenblatt*, Beiheft, October–December, 1847.
Anonymous, "Petite Guerre," *Encyclopédie*, XII, Paris, 1765.
Anonymous, *Rückzug der Franzosen*, St. Petersburg [Berlin], 1813.
Behrens, C.A.B., "Which Side Was Clausewitz on?" *New York Review of Books*, October 14, 1976.
Bloch, Marc, *Die seltsame Niederlage*, ed. Ulrich Raulff, Frankfurt, 1992.
———, *Mélanges historiques*, I, Paris, 1963.
———, *Strange Defeat*, trans. Gerard Hopkins, Oxford, 1949.
Bonjour, Edgar, *Studien zu Johannes von Müller*, Basel, 1957.
Briefe von und an Hegel, ed. Johannes Hoffmeister, III, Hamburg, 1954.
Brown, Hilda Meldrum, *Heinrich von Kleist*, Oxford, 1998.
Bülow, Eduard von, *Heinrich von Kleists Leben und Briefe*, Berlin, 1848.
Bülow, Heinrich von, *Lehrsätze des neuern Krieges*, Berlin, 1805.
Carus, Friedrich August, *Psychologie*, I and II, Leipzig, 1823.
Clausewitz, Carl von, "Bemerkungen über die reine und angewandte Strategie des Herrn von Bülow," *Neue Bellona* 9, no. 3 (1805).
———. "Der Feldzug von 1812 in Russland," *Hinterlassene Werke über Krieg und Kriegführung*, VII, Berlin, 1835.
———, "Die Feldzüge Friedrichs des Grossen von 1741–1762," *Hinterlassene Werke über Krieg und Kriegführung*, X, Berlin, 1837.
———, *Geist und Tat*, ed. Walter M. Schering, Stuttgart, 1941.
———, "Gustav Adolphs Feldzüge von 1630–1632," *Hinterlassene Werke des Generals Carl von Clausewitz über Krieg und Kriegführung*, IX, Berlin, 1837.
———, *Historical and Political Writings*, ed. and trans. Peter Paret and Daniel Moran, Princeton, 1992.
———, "Historische Briefe über die grossen Kriegsereignisse im Oktober 1806," *Minerva*, I and II (January, February, and August 1807).
———, *Historische Briefe über die grossen Kriegsereignisse im Oktober 1806*, ed. Joachim Niemeyer, Bonn, 1977.
———, *Nachrichten über Preussen in seiner grossen Katastrophe;* Kriegsgeschichtliche Einzelschriften, X, Berlin, 1888.
———, *On War*, ed. and trans. Michael Howard and Peter Paret, Princeton, 1976, rev. ed. 1984.

———, *Politische Schriften und Briefe,* ed. Hans Rothfels, Munich, 1922.
———, *Principles of War,* trans. and ed. Hans Gatzke, Harrisburg, 1942.
———, *Schriften–Aufsätze–Studien–Briefe,* ed. Werner Hahlweg, *Deutsche-Geschichtsquellen des 19. und 20. Jahrhunderts,* I–III, Göttingen, 1966–1990.
———, *Strategie aus dem Jahr 1804, mit Zusätzen von 1808 und 1809,* ed. Eberhard Kessel, Hamburg, 1937.
———, "Über das Leben und dem Charakter von Scharnhorst," *Historisch-Politische Zeitschrift,* I, 1832.
———, *Übersicht des Feldzugs vom Jahre 1813,* Leipzig, 1813.
———, *Vom Kriege, Hinterlassene Werke über Krieg und Kriegführung,* I–III, Berlin, 1832–1834.
Croix, de la, *Traité de la petite guerre,* Paris, 1752.
Delbrück, Hans, *Historische und politische Aufsätze,* Berlin, 1887.
Eichendorff, Joseph von, *Werke und Schriften,* IV, ed. Gerhart Baumann and Siegfried Grosse, Darmstadt, 1958.
Eloesser, Arthur, *Heinrich von Kleists Leben, Werke und Briefe,* Leipzig, n.d.
Emmerich, Andrew, *The Partisan in War,* London, 1789.
Epstein, Klaus, *The Genesis of German Conservatism,* Princeton, 1966.
Ewald, Johannes von, *Abhandlung von dem Dienst der leichten Truppen,* Leipzig, 1790.
Feilchenfeld, Konrad, *Varnhagen von Ense als Historiker,* Amsterdam, 1970.
Fink, Carol, *Marc Bloch: A Life in History,* Cambridge, 1989.
Fischer, R. von, "Die Feldzüge der Eidgenossen diesseits der Alpen...," *Schweizer Kriegsgeschichte,* I, ed. M. Feldmann and H. G. Witz, Bern, 1915.
Frederick the Great, "Mémoires pour servir à l'histoire de la Maison de Brandebourg," *Œuvres de Frédéric le Grand,* I, ed. J.-D.-E. Preuss, Berlin, 1846.
Gersdorff, Bernhard von, *Ernst von Pfuel,* Berlin, 1981.
Gilbert, Felix, *History: Politics or Culture?* Princeton, 1990.
Grandmaison, M. de, *La petite guerre ou traité du service des troupes légères en campagne,* Paris, 1756.
Grosser Generalstab, ed., *Das Preussische Heer der Befreiungskriege,* I, *Das Preussische Heer im Jahr 1812,* Kriegsgeschichtliche Abteilung II, Berlin, 1812.
Gundolf, Friedrich, *Anfänge Deutscher Geschichtsschreibung,* Amsterdam, 1938.
———, *Heinrich von Kleist,* Berlin, 1922.
Heuser, Beatrice, *Reading Clausewitz,* London, 2002.
Hinderer, Walter, *Schiller und kein Ende,* Würzburg, 2009.
———, "Zweideutige Machtspiele im Hause Brandenburg," *Heinrich von Kleist, Prinz Friedrich von Homburg,* Program Booklet of the Salzburger Festspiele, Salzburg, 2012.
Hintze, Otto, *The Historical Essays of Otto Hintze,* ed. Felix Gilbert, New York, 1975.
Höhn, Reinhard, *Revolution–Heer–Kriegsbild,* Darmstadt, 1944.
Jamme, Christoph, *Die Jahrbücher für wissenschaftliche Kritik,* Stuttgart–Bad Cannstadt, 1994.
Jamme, Chistoph, and Otto Pöggeler, *Johannes von Müller—Geschichtsschreiber der Goethezeit,* Schaffhausen, 1986.
Kleist, Heinrich von, *Germania an ihre Kinder,* ed. Georg Minde-Pouet, Berlin, 1918.
———, *Phöbus,* ed. Helmut Sembdner, Darmstadt, 1961.
———, *Prinz Friedrich von Homburg,* ed. Richard Samuel and Dorothea Coverlid, Berlin, 1964.
———, *Selected Writings: Heinrich von Kleist,* ed. and trans. David Constantine, London, 1997.
———, and Michael Kohlhaas, *Sämtliche Werke,* ed. Arthur Eloesser, IV, Leipzig, n.d.

Klippel, Georg Heinrich, *Das Leben des Generals von Scharnhorst*, I–III, Leipzig, 1869–71.
Kreutzer, Hans Joachim, *Heinrich von Kleist*, Munich, 2011.
———, "... und Frieden ist die Bedingung doch von allem Glück," *Jahrbuch der Bayerischen Akademie der Schönen Künste*, X, Munich, 1996.
Leebaert, Derek, *To Dare to Conquer*, Boston, 2007.
Lehmann, Max, *Scharnhorst*, Leipzig, 1886.
Lyon, Bryce, "Marc Bloch: Did He Repudiate *Annales* History?" *Journal of Medieval History* 11 (1985).
Meinecke, Friedrich, *Die Entstehung des Historismus*, Munich, 1946.
Mommsen, Katharina, *Kleists Kampf mit Goethe*, Heidelberg, 1974.
Müller, Johannes von, *Geschichten Schweizerischer Eidgenossenschaft*, rev. ed. I–IV, Leipzig, 1825–1826.
Müller, Johannes, *Die Geschichten der Schweizer*, Boston [Schaffhausen], 1780.
Niemeyer, Joachim, "Carl Ludwig Heinrich von Tiedemann," *Altpreussische Biographie*, IV, Marburg, 1984.
Nipperdey, Thomas, *Deutsche Geschichte, 1800–1866*, Munich, 1984.
———, *Deutsche Geschichte, 1866–1918*, Munich, 1993.
Paret, Peter, "Aufklärung und Preussische Reform: Clausewitz' Vorlesungen über den Kleinen Krieg," in *Ideenpolitik– Festschrift für Herfried Münkler*, ed. Harald Bloom, Karsten Fischer, and Marcus Llanque, Berlin, 2011.
———, "Bemerkungen zu dem Versuch von Clausewitz zum Gesandten in London ernannt zu werden," *Jahrbuch für die Geschichte Mittel- und Ostdeutschlands* 26 (1977).
———, "Clausewitz: A Bibliographical Survey," *World Politics* 17 (January 1965).
———, "Clausewitz and the Nineteenth Century," *The Theory and Practice of War*, ed. Michael Howard, London, 1965.
———, *Clausewitz and the State*, New York, 1976, rev. and expanded editions Princeton, 1985, 2007.
———, "Clausewitz: Half against My Will I Have Become a Professor," *Journal of Military History* 75 (April 2011).
———, "Kleist und Clausewitz," *Festschrift für Eberhard Kessel zum 75. Geburtstag*, ed. Heinz Duchardt and Manfred Schlenke, Munich, 1982.
———, *The Cognitive Challenge of War*, Princeton, 2009.
———, "Fontane und der nicht gegenwärtige Clausewitz," *Fontane Blätter* 69 (2000).
———, *Understanding War: Essays on Clausewitz and the History of Military Power*, Princeton, 1992.
———, *Yorck and the Era of Prussian Reform*, Princeton, 1966.
———, and John W. Shy, *Guerrillas in the 1960s*, New York, 1961.
Priesdorff, Kurt von, *Soldatisches Führertum*, IV–V, Hamburg, 1937.
Raulff, Ulrich, *Ein Historiker im 20. Jahrhundert: Marc Bloch*, Frankfurt, 1995.
Rothfels, Hans, *Carl von Clausewitz: Politik und Krieg*, Berlin, 1920; reprinted Bonn, 1980.
Rühle von Lilienstern, Johann Jakob, "Aphorismen über Kriegskunst, Kriegswissenschaft, Kriegsgeschichte," *Pallas* II (1809–10).
———, "Baron de Jomini: Introduction à l'étude ... de la stratégie et de la tactique," *Jahrbücher für wissenschaftliche Kritik* nos. 45–47 (March 1831).
———, *Bericht eines Augenzeugen von dem Feldzuge der während den Monaten September und Oktober ... Königl. Preussischen und Kurfürstl. Sächsischen Truppen*, Tübingen, 1807.
———, "Grundsätze der reinen Strategie," *Pallas* II (1809–10).
———, *Hieroglyphen oder Blicke aus dem Gebiete der Wissenschaft in die Geschichte des Tages*, Dresden, 1808.

———, *Reise mit der Armee im Jahre 1809*, I–III, Rudolstadt, 1810–1811.

———, *Vom Kriege. Ein Fragment aus einer Reihe von Vorlesungen über die Theorie der Kriegskunst*, Frankfort a. M., 1814.

———, "Vom Kriege. Hinterlassenes Werk des Generals Carl v. Clausewitz," *Jahrbücher für wissenschaftliche Kritik*, nos. 26–28 (August 1833).

Scharnhorst, Gerhard Johann David von, *Scharnhorst-Briefe an Friedrich von der Decken, 1803–1813*, ed. Joachim Niemeyer, Bonn, 1987.

———, *Scharnhorsts Briefe*, I, ed. Karl Linnebach [the second volume never appeared], Munich, 1914.

———, *Handbuch für Offiziere in den anwendbaren Theilen der Krieges-Wissenschaften*, I–III, Hanover, 1787–1790.

———, *Militärische Schriften*, ed. Colmar von der Goltz, Dresden, 1891.

———, *Militärisches Taschenbuch zum Gebrauch im Felde*, Hanover, 1792.

———, *Verfassung und Lehreinrichtung der Akademie für junge Offiziere, und des Instituts für die berlinische Inspektion*, Berlin, 1805.

Schib, Karl, *Johannes von Müller*, Schaffhausen, 1967.

Schiller, Friedrich von, *Ausgewählte Werke*, IV, ed. Ernst Müller, Darmstadt, 1954.

Schlieffen, Alfred von, *Friedrich der Grosse*, Berlin, 1927.

———, *Gesammelte Schriften*, I and II, Berlin, 1913.

———, ed., Carl von Clausewitz, *Vom Kriege*, Berlin, 1927.

Schwarz, Karl, *Leben des Generals Carl von Clausewitz …*, I and II, Berlin, 1878.

Sembdner, Helmut, *Heinrich von Kleists Lebensspuren*, Bremen, 1957.

Stadelmann, Rudolf, *Scharnhorst: Schicksal und geistige Welt*, Wiesbaden, 1952.

Staël, Anne-Louise-Germaine de, *De l'Allemagne*, Paris, 1810.

Tressac, M. de, "Guerre," *Encyclopédie*, VII, Paris, 1765.

Unger, Wilhelm von, *Blücher*, I and II, Berlin, 1908.

Valentini, Georg Wilhelm von, *Die Lehre vom Krieg*, I–II, Berlin, 1820–1822.

Venzky, Gabriele, *Die Russisch-Deutsche Legion in den Jahren 1811–1815*, Wiesbaden, 1966.

Waldman, Thomas, *Clausewitz and the Trinity*, Farnham, 2013.

White, Charles Edward, *The Enlightened Soldier*, New York, 1989.

Index of Texts

Anonymous
    Articles on Clausewitz, 57–58
Bloch
    Strange Defeat, 113–15, 119–25
Clausewitz
    Articles on 1806, 34, 113, 116
    Campaigns of Frederick, 77, 81–85
    early historical and other writings, 12, 24, 33, 72n9, 79–81, 92–97
    Lectures on the Little War, 35, 47, 81, 100–11
    Memorial of Confession, 48–49, 50, 105
    Observations on Prussia, 113–15, 117–19, 122–25
    On War, 5–17n4, 46–7, 58–64, 67–71, 74n43, 77, 78–79, 81–82, 85, 93–97, 102–3, 109–10
    Principles of War, 34–35
    Review of Bülow, 33–34, 47
Kant
    Critique of Knowledge, 32
Kleist
    The Prince of Homburg, 41–47, 70–71
    writings, 36–9, 41, 50
Müller
    History of the Swiss, 88–97
Rühle
    Review of On War, 58–63
    writings, 34, 36–41, 51–52, 53–54, 64, 97
Scharnhorst
    writings, 19, 22, 24, 25, 51, 108

Name Index

August, Prince of Prussia, 32, 34, 58

Bernadotte, Jean-Baptiste, Prince of Ponte-Corvo, later King Charles XIV of Sweden, 39, 52, 53
Bernhard, Prince of Saxe-Weimar, 36, 39, 41
Bismarck, Otto von, 95
Bloch, Marc, 114, 115, 119–25
Blücher, Gebhard Lebrecht von, 51, 52, 53, 55, 57
Bodmer, Johann Jakob, 89
Borstell, Karl Leopold von, 54
Boyen, Hermann von, 26
Brockhaus, Friedrich, 57
Brühl, Karl Friedrich von, 42
Brühl, Marie von (Marie von Clausewitz), 29, 101
Bülow, Dietrich Adam von, 11, 33, 34, 36, 47, 57

Carlyle, Thomas, 83
Charles, Archduke of Austria, 42
Charles VI, Emperor of Austria, 82
Clausewitz family, 28, 113–14
Clausewitz, Marie von, 16, 26, 42, 58
Condorcet, Marie Jean de, 122
Croix, de la, 107, 108

Davout, Louis-Nicolas, Prince of Eckmühl, 53
Decken, Johann Friedrich von der, 71n3
Diebitsch, Hans Carl von, 50

Ferdinand, Prince of Prussia, 29
Frederick, Prince of Homburg, 41, 42
Frederick William, Elector of Brandenburg, 42

Frederick II, King of Prussia, 14, 18, 21, 28, 29, 40, 42, 46, 60, 68, 77, 80–85, 88, 90, 107
Frederick William II, King of Prussia, 28
Frederick William III, King of Prussia, 26, 30, 35, 41, 42, 45, 49, 50, 54, 56, 92
Frederick William IV, King of Prussia, 65

Gilbert, Felix, 89
Gneisenau, August Wilhelm Neidhardt von, 26, 46, 48, 49, 51, 54, 55, 56, 58, 100
Goethe, Johann Wolfgang von, 21, 36, 37, 40, 59, 88, 95
Goltz, Colmar von der, 25
Grandmaison de, 107, 108
Grouchy, Emanuel de, 55
Gundolf, Friedrich, 46, 89
Gustavus Adolphus, King of Sweden, 24, 79, 80, 82

Hahlweg, Werner, 101, 105, 106, 108, 109
Haller, Albrecht von, 89
Hannibal, 84
Haugwitz, Christian August von, 118
Hegel, Georg Wilhelm Friedrich, 58, 59
Herder, Johann Gottfried, 88
Heuser, Beatrice, 71n3
Hitler, Adolf, 121
Hohenlohe, Prince Friedrich Ludwig, 32, 34
Hopkins, Gerard, 120
Humboldt, Wilhelm von, 59

Jomini, Antoine-Henri de, 11, 47, 64, 77

Kaminski, Gen., 34
Kant, Immanuel, 8, 16, 18, 31–2, 54
Kiesewetter, Johann Gottfried, 18, 31, 32

Name Index

Kleist, Heinrich von, 26, 27–28, 29, 30–31, 33, 34, 35, 36–39, 40, 41, 42–47, 50, 51, 55, 57, 64, 66, 68, 70–71
Knesebeck, Karl Friedrich von dem, 38, 39, 51, 56, 58
Kreutzer, Hans Joachim, 37
Kutusov, Prince Michael Laironovich, 49, 52

Lavater, Johann Caspar, 89
Levin, Rahel, 30

Macdonald, Jacques, Duke of Tarente, 50, 100
Machiavelli, Niccolò, 92
Mackensen, August von, 84
Massenbach, Christian von, 32, 34
Meinecke, Friedrich, 90
Montesquieu, Charles-Louis de Secondat de la Brède et de, 8, 89, 122
Müller, Adam, 36
Müller, Johannes von, 88–92, 93, 94–97

Napoleon I, Emperor of France, 10, 11, 14, 33, 40, 47, 50, 52, 53, 54, 55, 60, 77, 80, 81, 83, 85, 88, 92, 93, 94, 101, 118, 119, 125
Ney, Michel, Prince de La Moskowa, 41
Nipperdey, Thomas, 84

Pfuel, Ernst Adolf Heinrich von , 27, 28, 29, 30, 31,33, 34, 36, 38, 39, 40, 41, 50, 51, 53, 54, 55, 56, 57, 59, 64, 65, 66

Ranke, Leopold von, 63, 89

Rauch, Christian Daniel, 21
Raulff, Ulrich, 126n20
Rousseau, Jean-Jacques, 87
Rüchel, Ernst Friedrich von, 29, 46, 118, 126n15
Rühle von Lilienstern, Johann Jakob, 26, 27, 29–30, 31, 32–33, 34, 36, 39–40, 47, 51–52, 53–54, 55–56, 57, 58–64, 66, 67, 69, 97

Scharnhorst, Gerhard Johann David von, 12, 16, 18, 19–26, 29, 32, 33, 34–35, 36, 40, 46, 47, 48, 51, 53, 56, 57, 60, 69, 71n1–3, 81, 100, 101, 107, 108
Schiller, Friedrich von, 79, 80
Schlieffen, Alfred von, 83–85
Schmettau, Friedrich Wilhelm von, 34
Seeckt, Hans von, 84–85
Servan de Gerbey, Joseph, 87
Staël, Anne-Louise-Germaine de, 88

Thielmann, Johann Adolph von, 54, 55
Tiedemann, Carl Ludwig Heinrich von, 26, 27–28, 32, 34, 35–36, 40, 46, 47, 49, 56, 66, 100, 102, 104
Tressac, Marquis de, 112n1
Wallenstein, Albrecht von, 79
Wallmoden-Gimborn, Ludwig Georg von, 53
Wellington, Arthur Wellesley, Duke of, 55
William, Prince of Prussia, 65
William, Princess, 41
Willisen, Karl Wilhelm von, 64

Yorck, Hans David Ludwig von, 46, 50, 79